# DANGER AND OPPORTUNITY

# DANGER AND OPPORTUNITY

## BY RALPH PELCOVITZ

SHENGOLD PUBLISHERS, INC.

*New York City*

ISBN 0-88400-047-8

Library of Congress Catalog Card Number: 76-47304

Copyright © 1976 by Ralph Pelcovitz

All rights reserved

Published by Shengold Publishers, Inc.
45 W. 45th St., New York, N.Y. 10036

Printed in the United States of America

TO MY BELOVED WIFE

FRUMI

Who has been my true Ezer. A constant, loving, loyal source of support, encouragement and inspiration.

# Table of Contents

| | |
|---|---|
| Preface | 7 |
| **PART I** | |
| **AMERICAN ORTHODOXY** | |
| Introduction | 11 |
| 1. Who is the Orthodox Jew? | 13 |
| 2. American Orthodoxy — An Appraisal | 19 |
| 3. The Dilemma of Diversity and Unity | 26 |
| 4. Day Schools, Yeshivoth and the Community | 39 |
| 5. The Rabbi and the Rosh Yeshiva | 45 |
| 6. The Yeshiva Alumnus and the Synagogue | 51 |
| 7. A Manual for Baale Battim | 60 |
| **PART II** | |
| **ISSUES OF OUR TIME** | |
| Introduction | 71 |
| 8. Rebels — Because . . . | 73 |
| 9. The Lost Art of Derech Eretz | 83 |
| 10. Patterns of Morality | 90 |
| 11. Ecology and Jewish Theology | 100 |
| 12. Women's Lib in Torah Perspective | 111 |
| 13. The Intermarriage Problem | 123 |
| **PART III** | |
| **ISRAEL** | |
| Introduction | 137 |
| 14. The Reality of Galut | 139 |
| 15. Land of Promise, Fulfillment and Frustration | 141 |
| 16. Days of Trial, Triumph and Awe | 153 |
| 17. Israel's State of War — Israel's State of Mind | 161 |
| 18. Response to the Yom Kippur War | 168 |
| 19. Zionism, Judaism, and Eretz Yisroel | 177 |

# Acknowledgements

A number of chapters which appear in this book have been published in the form of articles in various publications during the past number of years. I wish to acknowledge with thanks permission granted by JEWISH LIFE, THE JEWISH OBSERVER and THE JEWISH PARENT. I have made a number of revisions to up-date their relevancy without altering or amending their basic thrust since the themes treated are, in my opinion, not dated. I have in some instances added comments which are germane and timely, motivated by a second look, thereby lending currency and relevancy.

I wish to acknowledge with heartfelt thanks and gratitude the assistance lent to me by my office staff, friends, congregants and pupils who have made the publication of this book possible. May the Almighty reward them with Kol Tov and may their greatest satisfaction be in the knowledge that they have helped in the wider dissemination of Torah true teachings.

A special 'Yasher Koach' is extended to Morton Fried, who is serving as President of my Congregation as I celebrate my 25th Anniversary with this distinguished Kehilla. Morton assumed the full responsibility for preparing the repro pages for this volume and his administration has generously underwritten the publication of this book in honor of my Silver Jubilee. May he and his fellow officers be blessed with health, happiness and prosperity in the merit of this wonderful gesture of friendship and esteem. I pray we all be granted many more fruitful years together.

# Preface

The word crisis is a most interesting one, charged with meaning and possessing a variety of interpretations. It refers to an unstable or crucial time and state of affairs. It also means the decisive moment, a turning point signifying a radical change of status in a person's, or a people's life. These definitions are most appropriate and correct in describing the times in which we live as members of the human race and particularly as Jews.

There is another interpretation of the word crisis based upon the Chinese method of writing wherein pictures and images represent words. The word crisis is written in the form of two characters, one representing danger the other opportunity. Each critical moment, every era of decision presents two faces — one fraught with danger, the other a favorable juncture of circumstances with chance for progress, the true meaning of the word opportunity.

When we observe the swift currents of change in the American Jewish community during the past decades, one is struck by the aptness of this latter definition. True we have lived through a succession of crises affecting the foundations of society, its morals and mores, its values and standards, but we have also come to appreciate the opportunities, as well as the dangers, which these crises present. Defection from Judaism and desertion from the Jewish community, carrying with it so much disillusion and despair, has also spurred the more sensitive to return to their traditional roots. The erosion of ethics morality and modesty has its built in backlash, witnessing in certain circles a rejection of materialism and a renewal of a sense of *tzenius*, an appreciation of purity without prudery.

The focus on ecology has aroused an interest in Judaism's

viewpoint, which is also the case regarding Women's Lib and other contemporary issues. Israel constantly presents its problems and promise, its frustrations and fulfillment and unending moments of crisis. There are also critical choices confronting the Jewish community internally. To mention but a few, the changing status and role of the rabbi and the Synagogue; the increasing intellectual growth, awareness and sophistication of baale baatim; the burgeoning of the day school movement and the relationship between the orthodox and non-orthodox communities are topics which require study and sober analysis. The emerging new breed of *bnai* Torah, the increasing influence of Roshei Yeshiva and the divisions within orthodoxy are also topics which demand our attention.

All these problems are critical in the sense that their solutions will be decisive in shaping the future of the Jewish community for decades to come while at the same time presenting us with opportunities to bring new vitality and strength to the Jewish community. A new paradoxical image is emerging, on the one hand a strange disquieting and bleak one of Jewish ignorance, apathy and assimilation while on the other a bright hopeful and promising one of increased Jewish knowledge, commitment and observance. Indeed these are times of crisis — of danger and opportunity.

The purpose of this book is to examine these critical problems and issues from a Torah perspective in the hope that the reader will be instructed even when he may be irritated but above all that he be provoked to think and reach intelligent conclusions on his own. It is our fervent prayer and hope that these essays will increase the reader's appreciation of Torah, grant new insights into the eternal wisdom of Judaism and strengthen one's loyalty and devotion to the Almighty and Israel — the people and the land. The unity of theme in these diverse and varied chapters is the basic one expressed in the classic statement of our Sages, "Israel, Torah and the Almighty are one".

# Part I

# American Orthodoxy

Introduction

# Between Despair and Euphoria

Orthodoxy in the United States has for many years fluctuated between the disparate poles of euphoria and despair. When we were told most emphatically by our heterodox brethren a half century ago that orthodoxy in this country was doomed we believed them. They were so self-assured and emphatic in their analysis and we in turn were frank enough to recognize signs of decline and decay within our community. As time passed, however, and these dire prophecies did not materialize and we began to detect a resurgence and vibrancy in the orthodox community we tended to proclaim that not only were we on the ascendancy but that other camps would eventually be phased out and we would inherit the future. This euphoric attitude was as exaggerated and incorrect as the spirit of despair which marked the earlier half of the twentieth century. The truth obviously lies somewhere in the middle. There is a beautiful Medrash regarding the *akedah* (the Binding of Isaac) which is most appropriate to this ambivalent attitude of American orthodoxy. When Abraham approached Mt. Moriah on the third day of his journey he asked Eliezer and Ishmael, "what do you see", to which they answered "wasteland and desolation". When Isaac was asked the same question, he replied "I see a beautiful mountain with a cloud hovering over it". For many decades, since the turn of the century when intelligent observers were asked what they foresaw for Orthodox Judaism in this country, many answered desolation and wasteland. How could the strictures of orthodoxy, its self-imposed isolation and its demands and disciplines survive in an open society as a minority within a minority, they argued. When a new generation established day schools and synagogues and founded communities reinforced by the influx of traditional Jews and spiritual leaders in the 1940's, there were many who saw the future of America reflected in their own limited and unique communities. The wasteland was being transformed into a garden. Both were, however, incorrect for the realistic reading of American orthodoxy's position and status is best described by Isaac's answer. There are many obstacles as forbidding and foreboding as a mountain with a cloud hovering over it, but it is a challenge that can be, and is being confronted by far more people than had been envisioned a generation or two ago. Those who have scaled the mountain and reached the top have also found that the view is quite beautiful and breathtaking.

Orthodoxy in this country has been much maligned because it has been greatly misunderstood. Because attitudes and opinions are shaped to such a great extent by the media, orthodoxy which has suffered from a bad press for decades has projected a distorted image. It is, therefore, imperative to define ourselves to others — who we are, how we function, what are our accomplishments, our dreams, our triumphs and failures. Above all, it is imperative to have the Jewish community appreciate what the Torah community means to them, its role as guarantor for the future.

These chapters are designed to define the orthodox Jew, to examine the image projected by orthodoxy and to analyze the relationship of the orthodox community to the heterodox one. In our study of the orthodox community the role played by the synagogue and yeshivos is of paramount importance as is the interrelationship with pulpit rabbi and Rosh Yeshiva. In recent years the synagogue has passed through a fundamental metamorphosis while the position of the rabbi and the rosh yeshiva have been profoundly affected by the growth of yeshivos and the infusion of yeshiva graduates into the orthodox community. Conflicts, tensions and problems have resulted which demand our attention and evaluation.

# Chapter 1

# Who is the Orthodox Jew?

Realistically speaking, in our Jewish communities of the United States and Canada the designation "orthodox Jew" is not necessarily applied only to those whose lives are built on observance of Jewish tenets. Certainly this designation is applicable essentially to the *Shomer Mitzvoth* and this orthodox Jew is, in number and capacity, the substantive element of the traditional Jewish world. Yet we must also include in the category of orthodox Jew the one who, while of lesser or even negligible observance in personal life, nevertheless retains spiritual allegiance to traditional Judaism. He is not a practicing orthodox Jew but rather a preferring one. He prefers to identify with the faith of his fathers and, in terms of formal affiliation, with the orthodox synagogue and community. In his case, it is a state not of being, but of believing — and yet loyalty, preference, and affiliation are the bearers of hope and promise, and the forerunners of the Mitzvah-dedicated life. The Jew who violates basic principles of faith but who cares about these principles, whose transgression is coupled with concern, is indeed entitled to be considered as an orthodox Jew within the framework of modern-day Jewish society.

Today, more so than in past decades the *Shomrey Mitzvoth* flourish in number and proportion, and play an important role on the overall Jewish scene. Yet along with the Shomer Mitzvoth is to be found, everywhere, that other, non-observant category of orthodox Jew. This category may well represent today a substantial segment of those designated "orthodox Jews." The type is not unique; in many communities it is the characteristic one. Out of its ranks, however, has emerged in recent years, and continues to emerge with increasing pace, yet another type of orthodox Jew. This one represents, if not yet the ideal, certainly a purposeful movement in the proper direction, aiming for the proper goal — belief translated into practice, observance based upon commitment, rather than nostalgia or sentiment.

In this age of choice, of option and opportunity, and yet an age marked by forces of conformity and assimilation with the prevalent culture, there have emerged varieties of orthodox Jews. We find the Jew whose orthodoxy is one of unbroken familial continuity in belief and practice: the Jew whose orthodoxy is as yet one of mere preference and affiliation: and the Jew — often from non-orthodox background — whose orthodoxy is one of voluntary, personal choice and commitment, born of his own spiritual searchings.

This last-named, as the first-named, orthodox Jew, might be described in capsule as one to whom Torah is not merely relevant to life but rather that which gives life relevance. Judaism, to him, is the fulfillment of the Teachings revealed by G-d to Israel at Sinai; timeless, all-encompassing, by which every area of life, every aspect of human endeavor, is to be directed and shaped. Indeed, that other orthodox Jew, the one of unfulfilled preference, also senses this truth and clings to it.

The orthodox Jew today, living as he does in an open society, buttressed though he be by his profound commitment to Torah Judaism, is confronted with problems basic to his distinctive situation: How shall he manifest his individual character? How shall he relate to the world and its manifold problems? How shall the collective character of the total orthodox Jewish community be manifested?

Foremost in his thinking is the realization that he must retain his identity as a committed Torah Jew while identifying himself with the general community. He must do this in a time marked by change, challenge, and persistent problems. In his Judaism he must be strong but never arrogant, tolerant without compromising his principles, reasoning while never rationalizing his beliefs.

Today's orthodox Jew must perforce live and function in two worlds. One is the world of Torah, the other society at large. In his relationship to society there must be awareness and concern; he cannot isolate himself from his surroundings. Yet his involvement must be measured and tempered by his special sense of values. He must ever judge, evaluate, and differentiate between the important demands of life and the lesser ones, the basic and the trivial. He must ever determine for what shall he sacrifice and what shall he relinquish. What do I *cherish* as opposed to what do I *admire*? What do I *need* as opposed to what do I *want*? These are the ever-recurring questions which pose themselves to the orthodox Jew living in a free, open society.

To answer these questions he must establish a sense and a scale of values. He must understand and accept that the Torah will fashion his values, his standards. The culture of the world may polish him, grant him sophistication, and give him tools and skills, yet it must never capture his soul or conquer his heart. It is a difficult and precarious balance that he must live with, but he must learn the lesson that an orthodox Jew may at times yield but never surrender. The Torah Jew immerses himself, his thinking, his attitudes, and his perspective, in the sea of Torah, but somehow can never plunge in with abandon into the ocean of ideas and values which the world around him offers.

This does not mean that the Torah Jew is unmindful of social challenges and worldly problems. On the contrary, he is most sensitive to them. He feels, however, that he must bring to these problems the Torah perspective, be it on civil rights, nuclear force, automation, or space conquest. The Torah-oriented approach and answer is for him correct and effective, for it flows from the source of the authentic Jewish spirit. The relevance of Torah to every area of human endeavor is to him a reality and most logical for it represents G-d's teachings and is appropriate for all time.

The two worlds in which the orthodox Jew lives represent constancy on the one hand and change on the other. Constancy represented in the eternal teachings and values of Torah, change in an environment that is revolutionized unceasingly by technological progress. Above all there is change in the shifting scale of values and standards of modern society. The vessels change, the Torah Jew must adapt, he must learn to use new tools and vehicles — all this while mindful of a goal that is constant and unchanging. He must live in a world of alien values and retain his identity. He must cherish the substance of Torah while the style and standards of society are in radical contrast to the dictates of Torah. He must reject isolation and detachment and yet not resign himself to total involvement. To walk this tightrope with balance, grace, and style is the challenge presented to the orthodox Jew in our century.

The individual identity of the orthodox Jew, manifested by means which we have described, must be matched by the manifestation of orthodoxy's collective identity. Just as an individual has a character and a soul so does a grouping, a community, a people have a collective soul and character. There must be a sense of purpose, experienced by a group, just as an individual realizes his need for a purpose and goal in life. To this end it is imperative that the voice and image of orthodoxy be projected with clarity, vigor, and imagination. We must be recognized by our sense of priority and by our scale of values. Our sensitivity and concern in areas such as Jewish education, communal responsibilities, philanthropy, Israel, and indeed every area of Jewish civic endeavor must be uniquely marked by the Torah spirit. The refinement of spirit and maturity of mind which Torah values implant in Torah Jews must be reflected in our every pronouncement and certainly in our policies. Here again our reverence for Torah manifests itself in making the Torah perspective relevant and meaningful at all times. Nothing in this world is alien or unimportant. The voice of orthodoxy must be recognized not because it is strident but because it is sincere and unequivocal.

In all frankness we must confess that our collective voice has often been muted and the collective identity of orthodox Jewry quite blurred. The future, however, may be a bit brighter if we appreciate our great potential and the strength that is ours.

"The influential" is the key phrase which will determine the destiny of Judaism in this country. Orthodox Jewry possesses within its ranks the "influentials." Our American culture, with its stress upon mass production, mass transportation, and mass media, has obscured the importance of the highly educated, the specialist, the expert, who, though a small minority, exert a great influence in the formation of public policy and opinion.

Perceptive political observers appreciate the impact of the intellectual upon society, subtle though it may be. The wise student of history realizes the power of the elite — quality which transcends quantity, caliber which surpasses cant and conformity. Sheer numbers may triumph for a time, but ultimately, it is the knowing, committed, and courageous carriers of ideas and ideals who prevail.

In the Jewish community, obsession with enrolled numbers, the yardstick of quantity and the measure of importance by size, has also been dominant in recent years, reflecting the values of society at large. This too, has obscured a vital truth. The strength, the power of growth, indeed the means of survival of Judaism and Jews in this country have not been manifested in forces and movements with the greatest organized numbers. The sad failure of major Jewish organizations — religious and secular — to stem the tide of assimilation, intermarriage, and increasing loss of Jewish identity, is directly responsible for the so-called "vanishing Jew." When authentic Judaism vanishes the Jew becomes invisible as well. The tenuous ties to Jewishness of a new generation, the blurred lines of demarcation between Jew and non-Jew, testify to the bankruptcy of groupings and organizations on the American Jewish scene which have centered on multiplication of number. This obsession with numbers has led, paradoxically, to an alarming decrease in numbers.

Orthodoxy has demonstrated in recent years that only total commitment to Torah Judaism can increase the quality and caliber of those whose latent loyalties are awakened. The revolutionary change wrought in the orthodox camp has been the increasing observance among younger people of Jewishness and Jewish practice, rooted in conviction rather than coercion, in deep belief rather than superficial sentimentality, in understanding rather than conformity. This elite, educated, qualitative force within Jewry, though not in mass number, must have its effect upon the complexion of communities. Their influence is already felt in many areas and will increasingly be sensed as the products of the day schools and yeshivoth take their rightful places in the American Jewish community. Responsible Jewish leaders are beginning to recognize this new breed of "influentials" — the intelligent, sophisticated, articulate, committed, orthodox Jew.

What is of equal importance is that important elements of the non-Jewish community, especially its religious leaders, are beginning to realize that they may have been conducting their dialogue with Jewish leaders who represent for the most part, the vanishing Jew. The next few years may well witness full recognition on the part of the general community, that the authentic Jewish spokesmen and leaders are those who speak on behalf of and represent authentic Judaism — namely, orthodox Judaism.

We see then, that the orthodox Jew, evolving from the affiliated to the committed, from preference to practice, must perforce function in two worlds. His values must be drawn from Torah while his skills and tools come from the halls of universities and his tastes and style are influenced by his environment. The world is very much with him, but he attempts to transcend it while remaining in it.

As for the orthodox Jewish community, its strength lies in its quality, its total commitment to functional Jewishness in depth as opposed to nostalgic and superficial cultism. Vanishing Jews are the direct result of vanishing Judaism. Orthodox Jews are ever-enduring ones for they are linked to eternal ideas and ideals. Not by numbers or *nissim*, but by constancy and courage will they prevail.

A number of years ago a political analyst said of a Western leader who was imperious yet perceptive, and whose intransigence presented problems to the Western alliance, that the trouble with the good general was that "one half of him is in the nineteenth century while the other is in the twenty-first century." The perceptive, positive orthodox Jew finds himself in this same dilemma. He is rooted in the traditions of the past while ever preparing for the future. He is attached to the past while seeing much more clearly than others what the future holds in store. His perspective is colored by the Sinai experience while his grasp and vision propel him far beyond the immediate tomorrow to the historic tomorrow of the Jewish people.

Jefferson once said: "Liberty is a boisterous sea. Timid men prefer the calm of despotism." Orthodoxy is also a boisterous sea, difficult, challenging, and exhilarating. Timid Jewish souls may prefer the convenient, the comfortable, the dull conformity of a safe, undemanding religion. It is our lot and historic destiny to be the guardians of the heritage which was entrusted to us. This is our destiny, especially in our day, not by virtue of self-designation but by virtue of our loyalty, our faith, by adherence and continuity. History will record whether we have the stamina and courage to sail this boisterous sea.

# Chapter 2

# American Orthodoxy — An Appraisal

Despite orthodoxy's growth and progress in recent years, we have still been unsuccessful in projecting a clear image of ourselves. We are the heirs of an insecure past resulting from the transplanting of a vibrant self-respecting and self-assured Torah community to a strange land, the United States, whose soil rejected initially these alien plantings and whose environment was inhospitable to the unique life style of traditional Jews. Orthodoxy in the early part of this century suffered from a sense of inferiority and its leadership, although well versed in Torah and Jewish law, was ill equipped to cope with the new world. This three-fold scourge of inadequacy, insecurity, and inferiority marked the early period of orthodoxy in the United States. The reasons for these problems can be sketched in a few brief paragraphs.

The huge wave of Jewish immigration to the United States, in the late nineteenth and early twentieth centuries, came from that fortress and bastion of Orthodox Judaism — eastern Europe. These hardy souls found America a bewildering and alien land where Torah observance was fraught with difficulties and nigh insurmountable obstacles. Eking out a living was of paramount importance. Security and social adjustment were the great challenges to be confronted and conquered — at any price. Unfortunately, the price was very high. Abandonment of Jewish practices and traditions, of Torah education and adherence to mitzvoth — this was the cruel medium of exchange, the coin of the realm — or so it seemed. The majority were willing to pay the price and the tenacious orthodox practicing minority were beleaguered and bewildered.

The means to combat this spiritual decline, and Jewish erosion, were woefully inadequate. This inadequacy in turn resulted in a painful sense of inferiority and insecurity in the Torah-true camp. The few fading champions of orthodoxy reluctantly admitted they were fighting a losing battle, where all their cherished hallowed practices and principles were rapidly being vanquished, and a new, modern, liberal Judaism was emerging victorious.

The optimists were limited in number, and even if they saw a light where it didn't exist there were pessimists who insisted upon rushing in to blow it out. To the delight, however, of these incurable optimists, and the dismay of persistent pessimists, the orthodox Jewish community refused to acknowledge their oft-issued death certificates, and, like that famous American humorist, demonstrated with time that their heralded demise was a gross exaggeration.

The present-day scene, though far from being one of all light and no shadows, is nonetheless a most heartening one. The years of faithful plantings in the Torah *chinuch* field are finally bearing fruit. American-born and -educated men and women have become the proud, vigorous standard bearers of Torah Judaism. The bleak winter of our disenchantment has given way to a new spring of hope and the voice of commitment to the traditional law is once again heard in the land.

Inadequacy has been replaced by adequate leadership, facilities, institutions, and organizations. A sense of status, prestige, and even fierce pride as Torah-oriented Jews has negated the sense of inferiority. The deep roots of happy, total Jewish living without conflicts, in the American community, have driven out the spectre of insecurity.

In spite of these strides, orthodoxy is beset by numerous problems which prevent its full development, and above all, its ability to reach out beyond its own limited circles. Primarily they have found it most difficult to alter their stereotyped image as it is projected into important circles of power, both internally and externally. The Jewish establishment, perhaps more so than the average Jew, finds it difficult to accept seriously the great progress made by orthodoxy in recent years and they have granted but begrudging limited recognition to its vibrancy and growth. How to overcome this deficiency by impressing upon Jewish leadership the awakening of many young men and women in urban and suburban areas to the challenge of Torah tradition is at the very top of orthodoxy's agenda.

The second problem is that of disunity in orthodoxy's ranks. Torah Jewry is obviously far from monolithic and its internal divisions are unfortunately increasing rather than decreasing as this community becomes stronger. There have been many fundamental changes and shifting of power within the orthodox community during the past two decades which the older entrenched orthodox establishment refuses at times to accept gracefully. These radical changes have moved at times in opposite directions. For example, the long established influential voice of the orthodox rabbinate, the Agudas Harabonim, has dwindled in size and lost its position of power while the Rabbinical Council of America and to a lesser degree the Rabbinical Alliance of America, comprised of younger, more modern rabbis, have attained positions of influence. Conversely, the Mizrachi Organization of America has rapidly been diminished in numbers, as well as influence, while the Agudath Israel which for years was looked upon as a small inconsequential right wing group has made great strides, increasing not only in numbers, but through its various agencies made a considerable impact upon the non-Jewish community, especially in government circles.

The third area which must be thoroughly examined, if one is to understand orthodoxy's position today, is that of its relationship to other Jewish religious groups. The question of Orthodoxy's participation in mixed (Conservative and Reform) rabbinic and synagogue organizations has caused a deep difference of opinion within the orthodox community. Involvement with non-observant Jews has ever presented problems, both practical and ideological, to the traditional Jew. Although he has found that he can comfortably join together with his fellow Jews in *k'lal Yisroel* endeavors, organizational affiliation in so-called umbrella groups which are religiously oriented has become a divisive and emotionally charged issue in recent years.

These three areas of (1) orthodoxy's impact upon the general community, (2) its internal fragmentation and (3) the question of its relationship with other Jewish religious groupings must be examined closely and appraised in the hope that it will help us reach clarification and decision.

Although the orthodox community is not large in number and certainly not the wealthiest group in American Jewry, nonetheless they represent, Jewishly speaking, a most vibrant, committed and promising segment of world Jewry. Assimilation, inter-marriage and Jewish ignorance, which has weakened the fabric of Jewish communities and threatens their very survival, is minimal among Torah committed Jews. Indeed they possess two virtues which represent the insurance of continuity and survival, namely, *commitment* and *concern*, which are tragically lacking among many of their secular and marginal-religious brethren.

Unfortunately, their voice, vital and vibrant as it may be, is a muted one and their image a blurred one largely ignored by the Jewish establishment and unknown in many influential circles. It is strange but true that those who offer the best hope of frustrating the "vanishing Jew" prophecy are the most invisible at the present time! In an age where the agenda of important issues is established by the media and priorities are pressed upon the public through this media, number, size and prominence is that which dictates what is newsworthy to them and what is of importance to the Jewish establishment.

This deficiency in communicating the growth and progress of a dynamic minority has characterized the orthodox community for many decades but there are some hopeful heartening signs (in the past decade or so) with the awakening of a sense of self-respect and self-assurance in the Torah camp. True, spokesmen for the Jewish community are still those who are not identified with traditional Jewry, and Jewish public funds are allocated to Torah institutions in the same trickle which marked past years, yet there is a new awareness in some circles, Jewish and governmental, that the orthodox community is one that merits their attention and sympathetic understanding.

In recent years we have become accustomed to the fact that without huge sums of government grants, major educational institutions cannot exist. We also take for granted the allocation of huge sums of Jewish public funds for Israel's needs, communal Jewish projects and service organizations. The amount, however, allocated toward Jewish education in general and Torah education in particular is still comparatively a pittance and in most cases scandalously inadequate. The dramatic growth of day schools and yeshivoth during the past two decades, the most productive phenomenon on the American Jewish scene, has only recently been reluctantly recognized by the Council of Jewish Federations and Welfare Funds. In spite of this new awareness, there still has been very slow progress in obtaining desperately needed funding by Federations throughout the United States. And this at a time of such financial crunch that many day schools and yeshivoth are on the brink of bankruptcy. Torah Umesorah has done an outstanding job in bringing the story of day schools and yeshivoth to American Jewry, but unfortunately with limited practical results. The scale of priorities is still tipped toward Israel and general communal Jewish needs and control of public Jewish purse strings is still in the hands of men and women whose sensitivity to, and appreciation of, Torah chinuch is minimal at best when it is not antagonistic.

One may argue that traditional Jewish education is of particular interest to a comparatively small grouping within the Jewish community and should therefore be their responsibility as opposed to needs which are general and total in nature, i.e., Israel, displaced Jews, and protection of Jewish rights. Others also point to the lack of appreciable orthodox participation in Federation activities and the disinterest shown by many of its leaders, rabbinic and lay, in their endeavors. These criticisms and complaints are not completely without merit but they do not justify the failure of Federation leadership to properly evaluate the primary need of our generation. The only historic proven guarantee of Jewish continuity and identity, which is certainly the concern of all Jews, is the proper education and training of each succeeding generation. Intermarriage, acculturation and assimilation, all fruits of Jewish ignorance and the erosion of Torah observance, has alarmingly diminished the Jewish community and therefore the ultimate question which must certainly plague Federation leadership is — who will be the contributors of the future? Self-interest dictates that Jewish public funds collected and disbursed by Federations throughout this country be channeled in large and meaningful amounts into Jewish education which will at least insure a significant number of knowledgeable, positive Jews who will ultimately raise and channel money for *all* Jewish causes. The orthodox community has unfortunately been unable to date to impress this vital message upon the established Jewish leadership.

It is not only in the area of Jewish public funds that orthodoxy is still unsuccessful in projecting its image and message but also in the arena of public affairs where its voice is often muted either by being submerged or by its inability to reach the broad public and its representatives since many channels of communication are unavailable to them. Whether the issue is government aid to private schools, liberalization of abortion laws, equal rights for women or the "Jewish" position on Vietnam, Watergate and civil rights, the self-appointed Jewish spokesman does not usually reflect Torah thinking, yet he presents himself as voicing the attitude and opinion of American Jewry.

For example, the impression was given through the media that Jewish opposition to the United States government's policy in Vietnam was nigh unanimous and their attitude toward President Nixon during the Watergate period deeply antagonistic. Radical and liberal Jewish spokesmen were so articulate and vociferous in presenting their viewpoint that it gave the impression that practically all Jews were as vitriolic in their attitudes, as they were, regarding the United States role in the Vietnam war. The truth is that the orthodox community was much milder in its opposition and at times even supportive of the administration's stance in pursuing a militant anti-communist policy in southeast Asia. In general, the orthodox community is a far more conservative one than the heterodox and much more militant in their opposition to communist ideology and expansion, knowing full well its effect upon religion in general, and Jewish observance in particular.

Nor was the orthodox community as vehement, as some of their liberal brothers, in the anti-Nixon crusade, mindful as they were of his strong support of Israel in 1973 and also due to the traditional spirit of Judaism which commands Jews to be respectful of authority and pray for the peace and stability of the government in whose land they dwell. During those eventful years the inability of orthodoxy to make its position clear served to underscore one of its great weaknesses: its failure to produce its own channels of communication and to cultivate its relationship with the media. This, in an age when it is so important to have access to all channels of communication if one's position is to be made known.

The Torah community has certainly far less contact with the church than do the Conservative and Reform clergymen. One of the ironies of recent years has been, however, that the Jewish champions of ecumenism (a movement rejected by Torah-true Jews who feel that its dangers outweigh its benefits) have antagonized the Catholic church by their militant stand on abortion reform and their strong opposition to government aid for parochial schools. All this while the orthodox community finds itself in strange alliance with the Catholic community on these issues! Here again is an example of the failure of Jewish secular and liberal religious groups to read the true temper of a sizeable segment of their own people while antagonizing a large Christian group they are attempting to court! Unfortunately, the impression given through the media is that the Jewish position on these issues is more or less monolithic and little attention is paid to the Orthodox Jewish position on these vital questions.

There has, however, been some progress in recent years, in Orthodoxy's attempt to articulate its own position and above all in utilizing legal means to achieve their ends. A national commission on law and public affairs, known as COLPA, co-founded by the U.O.J.C.A. and the Agudath Israel in 1966 has had outstanding success in protecting the rights of Sabbath observers and in combating anti-*shechitah* legislation. Agudath Israel has been very active in battling for Jewish rights and been successful in obtaining governmental aid for Yeshivoth even though the courts have cut off major aid. They have also been successful in obtaining recognition of Yeshivoth Gedoloth as institutions of higher learning, on an equal footing with colleges, by the United States Office of Education. The Union of Orthodox Jewish Congregations has certainly written a glorious chapter in the field of *kashruth*. During the past few decades kashruth has come of age with kosher food served on airlines and in hospitals as a matter of right and not as special privilege. More and more campuses have kosher dining halls for which the National Council of Young Israel can take much credit. Hillel Houses are far more responsive to the needs of orthodox students and manufacturers of food have become increasingly aware of the financial benefits which will accrue to them by having their products certified kosher. Hotels and resorts, heretofore insensitive to the dietary needs of observant Jews, have also become increasingly understanding of these requirements. In these respects orthodoxy has come a long way. It is clear, however, that the Torah voice will not be heard and the Torah community not fully understood until there will be unity in orthodoxy's own ranks.

# Chapter 3

# The Dilemma of Diversity and Unity

To those who are unacquainted with the United States orthodox community, unfamiliar with its institutions, personalities, life style and values, this Torah community appears to be a homogeneous, almost monolithic grouping. Most American Jews are aware of certain external differences; bearded and clean shaven rabbis, traditional and modern garbed men and women, imposing orthodox synagogues and store front *shtiblach*, but the overall picture presented is that of men and women committed to an observant way of life. They all seem to fit a mold of disciplined and dedicated Jews who stubbornly cling to their meticulous fulfillment of the *mitzvoth*, resisting the torrent of change which has washed away the special Jewish life style of the vast majority of American Jews. This is highly visible in their eating habits, Sabbath observance, synagogue attendance and the proliferation of yeshivoth and day schools in orthodox communities.

To those, however, who are familiar with American orthodoxy, privy to its multitude of variations and sensitive to the subtle and not so subtle differences within this important segment of American Jewry, the existence of fragmentation, friction and disunity is very real. Jewish history is replete with dissension and internal conflict since the time of Moses. Unfortunately, many of these profound differences, resulting in deep divisions, have been prevalent more so in the religious community. This is understandable since the protagonists are motivated by the fervor of their convictions and are positive of the righteousness of their cause. Jews, whose religious commitments are marginal are naturally tolerant of different points of view since their own commitments are comparatively superficial. The pious Jew, on the other hand is devoted and very serious in his religious convictions, thereby resulting in zealous and passionate defense of his particular position coupled with rejection of those who are considered deviationists.

Different degrees of piety, a variety of observance levels, disagreements regarding Jewish priorities and a dissimilar value system has resulted in the emergence of a number of camps within Orthodoxy. The Chasidic community and the yeshiva 'velt' (world) pursue their own unique paths, rarely converging. The Young Israel and modern orthodox synagogue world function in their circles, the Agudah pays scant attention to Mizrachi, except when they are moved to vigorously criticize them, and this attitude is reciprocated in turn, while the various rabbinical groups continue to act independently of each other. For those who are fond of neat, concise categories and recognizable delineations it would be fair to state that there are two major camps in American orthodoxy today. Each has its satellites while three national groups seem to fluctuate between the two camps. One major camp is the modern-liberal one dominated by Yeshiva University, the Rabbinical Council of America and the Mizrachi. The vast majority of so-called modern orthodox synagogues fall into their orbit. The second major camp is the Yeshiva world, Agudath Israel, together with the so-called right wing rabbinical groups, the b'nai Torah fraternity and the smaller numerous *shuls* and *shtiblach*. The three national organizations which bridge these two camps are the Union of Orthodox Jewish Congregations of America, Torah Umesorah and the Young Israel movement. The former is probably closer to the modern orthodox camp while the other two identify themselves more so with the traditional Torah one. True, it is imprecise and even dangerous to label and pigeonhole institutions, organizations and groups, nonetheless, anyone conversant with the spectrum of American orthodoxy today will grant that there are two distinct forces emerging. One, the modern-liberal and moderate camp, the other more traditional, conservative and yet at times more militant.

The areas where these two camps are of differing opinions are manifold. Torah chinuch, secular higher education, synagogue standards and social activities are among fundamental issues which divide these two forces. Zionism, the State of Israel, Soviet Jewry and the question of involvement with non-orthodox and secular organizations are also among the areas where significant deep differences of opinion exist.

Education has always been the number one priority for Jews since the emergence of the Jewish people. Our thirst for knowledge and desire to expand our scholastic horizons are legendary. To the Torah Jew, however, it is far more than the pursuit of knowledge and wisdom with a passion to excel. The Hebrew word for education — *chinuch* — reveals the added dimension in the *hashkafah* of the traditional Jew. It means training, dedication and sacred consecration to the study of G-d's Torah which is meant to be translated into observance of mitzvoth. "Great is study for it brings to deeds" is a rabbinic dictum that orthodox Jews accept fully and pursue most seriously. However, what the curriculum should be, where the emphasis should be placed and what form the school should take has divided American orthodox Jews for the past many years. Among the fundamental problems on the elementary and secondary level have been the questions of co-ed versus separate boys and girls schools and the primacy of pure Torah studies as opposed to a broader enriched curriculum which includes Hebrew language, literature, Jewish history and philosophy. On the college level the difference of opinion and the frictions which ensue is a twofold one. The commitment of Yeshiva University to the continuation of an integrated program of Torah and academic studies on the college level is anathema to the traditional yeshivoth. They are not only opposed to introducing college courses into the environs of the Beth Hamedrash but are also opposed, to a lesser or greater degree, to their students pursuing college studies in general.

Even when they permit their students to attend college (in the evening after a full day of Torah study) they often limit the time, number of credits and type of subjects. The extra-curricular activities of the yeshiva *bochur* are also curtailed and the Rosh Yeshiva does not conceal his displeasure with those who choose to pursue a college career instead of devoting their time exclusively to Torah study.

In the social activities arena we can also observe divergent approaches between the modern and traditional Yeshiva community. In modern yeshiva circles young men and women socialize freely and participate in various activities which are deemed to be halachically acceptable. In traditional-oriented yeshivoth these activities are prohibited and considered serious infractions of

## The Dilemma of Diversity and Unity

halacha and certainly incompatible with the Torah spirit. What is considered the norm in one camp is rejected as a negation of Torah law in the other. This is true regarding synagogue standards as well. The height of a *mechitza* separating the men and women in Shul, becomes a barrier between orthodox Jews in the community separating one observant Jew from his brother. Briefly these are but some of the differing practices and principles which divide orthodox Jewry internally. Ideologically there are even sharper differences of opinion within the Torah community. The differing attitudes toward Zionism, the State of Israel, Soviet Jewry and cooperation with non-orthodox Jewish institutions underscore dramatically the existence of two camps within orthodoxy. It is in these areas that the rift is deep and emotions run high.

The question of how to view the establishment of the State of Israel from the perspective of Torah has perplexed orthodox Jewry since 1948 in a manner which secular Jews find difficult to understand or appreciate. To a believing Jew, who examines Jewish history from a Torah perspective, many questions were projected with the establishment of the State. Is it the beginning of redemption, the first stirrings of the Messianic period or a test of Israel's faith in the Almighty, given the secular and even anti-religious character of the State and its leadership? Political Zionism, the forerunner of the State, was accepted by some in the orthodox camp as a necessary vehicle for the return to the Holy Land, leading eventually to the *geulah shelamah*, the full redemption. To many other orthodox Jews, however, it was considered an *avodah zarah*, a strange and alien nationalism, the antithesis of the Torah's concept of Jewish peoplehood as a nation of priests and a holy people. Hence the ongoing dispute in day schools, yeshivoth and synagogues regarding the religious celebration of Yom Ha"Atzmaut (Israel Independence Day), the display of the Israeli flag and the singing of Hatikvah at public assemblies or the acceptance of the Chief Rabbinate as the highest religious authority in Israel. United as they may be in doing all that is humanly possible to strengthen and secure the State of Israel, sparing no effort in defending it from its enemies and nurturing its growth, the two camps in orthodoxy are certainly divided in the degree of their allegiance to the State and their acceptance of its policies, programs and philosophies.

Soviet Jewry's plight concerns all Jews, and especially orthodox

## The Dilemma of Diversity and Unity

Jews who have been in the forefront of the battle for their survival, their freedom to emigrate, the right to observe their religion and retain their Jewish identity. How to work and fight on their behalf, however, is again a cause for dissension within orthodoxy. Quiet diplomacy or demonstrations? Should emigration and *aliyah* to Israel be given priority or is the wherewithal to live as observant Jews in Russia more important? Once they do come to Israel how involved should American orthodoxy be with their religious well-being and absorption in the Jewish State? What of the packages sent to the U.S.S.R. — should they go to the activists or to those who are struggling to keep Shabbos and give their children a Jewish education?

In all the areas mentioned there emerges a distinct diversity of opinion, and we do perceive, broadly speaking, two camps within orthodoxy. The modern-liberal one favoring an integrated program of Torah and general studies on all educational levels, a relaxed, tolerant attitude regarding social activities, fierce devotion to the State of Israel, and full cooperation with the established Jewish communities' activist program regarding Soviet Jewry. The traditional, more conservative camp within orthodoxy stresses not only the primacy of Torah study, which is accepted by all Torah-true Jews, but only begrudgingly recognizes the inevitable demands made by modern society on the yeshiva student to pursue his academic studies. They are strongly opposed to any relaxation of the traditional Jewish restraints in the social realm, frowning on dating and mixed socializing. Their support for the State of Israel is limited and guarded while their concern for Soviet Jewry is channeled into efforts to sustain their brethren in the U.S.S.R., helping them to fulfill their religious needs, and safeguard their religious well-being once they emigrate.

A caveat should be added at this point. Some of the differences regarding college, social practices, the State of Israel and Soviet Jewry are not always subscribed to by all those mentioned belonging to the two camps, respectively. Some of the so-called moderates in the liberal camp may be quite strict in their point of view, while some of the traditionalists in the more conservative camp may personally be more lenient.

The deepest cleavage in recent years within orthodoxy is manifested, however, in the area of inter-religious relationship,

## The Dilemma of Diversity and Unity

between the Torah community and the non-orthodox religious community. For many years orthodox rabbis and laymen have had great misgivings belonging to mixed rabbinate or synagogue groups. In general, if the character of an organization was a purely religious one it created doubts in the minds of orthodox rabbis and laymen more so than if the character of the group was a secular communal one. Historically Judaism has never recognized 'denominations' or 'wings' in the Protestant sense. Jews were either observant or not, they believed or denied, they were religionists or secularists but the Jewish faith community — its laws, practices and disciplines — was very clear and recognizable. The Almighty had given His people a Torah which represented the sum total of their faith and practice as interpreted by Oral Law and codified in the *Shulchan Aruch*. There had always been challenges to the supremacy and authority of Torah Law, indeed since the time of Korach and Moshe. Various sects have risen and fallen over the ages, the Sadducees and Karaites in particular. But not until the Reform movement in the 19th century did radical departure from authentic Jewish practice and belief subsequently become a denomination *within* Judaism. This was followed eventually by the Conservative interpretation of Judaism which also claimed its rights as a wing within the Jewish faith community.

The battle lines between Orthodoxy and Reform were established in Europe, when this movement emerged, but it was in this country where the battle was fully joined, initially between the same antagonists and later joined and intensified by the emergence of a strong Conservative movement. The early period of this conflict was one marked by a weak, ill-equipped, and meek Orthodox leadership whose unsure younger, modern spiritual leaders chose to accept the realities of 20th-century life. The American Jewish community, they argued, was one comprised of three denominations and it was important therefore to cooperate with the non-orthodox in such bodies as the Synagogue Council of America and various Boards of Rabbis. True, there were those in the orthodox rabbinate who resisted this pragmatism and refused to capitulate and join these organizations. This was due either to their distaste and discomfort or their conviction that participation in such groups would grant legitimacy and recognition to those whom they considered deviationists.

## The Dilemma of Diversity and Unity

The post-World War II period witnessed a resurgence of orthodox self-pride and an ever-increasing sense of self-confidence. The immigration of many devout Chasidic and East European Jews who had escaped the Nazis increased the numbers of orthodox Jews in urban areas. The arrival of Torah luminaries and their disciples coupled with the steady growth of yeshivoth brought a spirit of rejuvenation to the orthodox community. There was an increasing questioning of the wisdom of submerging the image of orthodoxy and muting its voice in Councils and Boards which equated all expressions of Judaism, be it one of Torah or those of recent vintage whose views and practices were completely alien to tradition. In 1956 this philosophy and spirit of militancy found its expression in the *Issur* (interdiction) of eleven leading Roshei Yeshiva prohibiting their pupils and followers from participating in mixed rabbinic and synagogue organizations. This Issur did not extend to secular or communal groups even though they included rabbinic or synagogue representatives, providing that these councils or conferences did not deal with religious matters but rather with k'lal Yisroel interests.

From the outset it was clear that this Issur would result in a deep and ever-widening rift within orthodoxy. Two major organizations continued their affiliations with the Synagogue Council of America, namely the Rabbinical Council of America and the Union of Orthodox Jewish Congregations. Many individual rabbis retained their membership in the New York Board of Rabbis. Realistically speaking, those who had never been members of these mixed groups continued their refusal to join but they now had sanction and support from these outstanding recognized Torah personalities. Twenty years later the two schools of thought have not moved from their initial positions. The modern-liberal camp is adamant in its determination to pursue a policy of participation while the traditional-conservative camp resolutely refuses to join the S.C.A. or N.Y.B.R. The U.O.J.C.A., one of the national groups mentioned above as bridging the two worlds of orthodoxy, has found itself buffeted and pressured incessantly by this issue and it remains a source of fragmentation and bitterness within its ranks. As the only orthodox congregational group in the Synagogue Council of America, the Union has been caught between two opposing forces. On the one hand, the R.C.A., their rabbinic arm and partner

## The Dilemma of Diversity and Unity

in a number of these mixed groups, keeps pressuring them to remain while, on the other, it has always been their policy to foster a closer relationship with the 'right wing' and Yeshiva world. This issue has been brought before conventions of the Union since 1956, reaching a climax in 1974 when the Board of the Union voted to suspend its membership in the S.C.A. in the aftermath of the "Who is a Jew?" controversy in the State of Israel.

This drastic decision on the part of the Union was triggered by the demand of the non-orthodox rabbinate that the Israeli government grant their conversions recognition equal to those of the orthodox. To support this demand they cited their joint participation in the Synagogue Council of America as proof of their legitimacy and acceptance of same by the orthodox rabbinate and the U.O.J.C.A. What exacerbated this inflammatory demand was the extent to which a number of Reform and Conservative leaders went, threatening to withhold support (U.J.A. and Bonds) from the State of Israel if recognition of their religious authority was denied! A vituperative campaign was also launched against the Chief Rabbinate and the National Religious Party in Israel. Convinced that these attacks, threats and demands were encouraged by the presence of orthodox groups in the S.C.A., the Union Board voted to suspend its membership, subject to the approval of its membership at their convention in November. The end of this episode is anti-climactic. The entire matter was sent back by the convention to the Board for final decision, with a brief detour to a joint commission comprised of the R.C.A. and the Union who were evenly divided on the issue. The Board in 1975 by a comparatively close vote decided to resume its membership in the S.C.A. and there the matter presently rests.

Many ask why this persistent continuing battle within orthodoxy regarding what seems to the average person to be a relatively unimportant issue. It is vital, however, to understand the symbolic seriousness and weight given to this question by both sides. Those who favor membership in the Synagogue Council of America, and to a lesser extent in the New York Board of Rabbis, fear a splitting away by orthodoxy from the rest of the Jewish community. They look upon any change in the status quo as an act of secession which will result in orthodoxy's isolation. Jewish unity is their overriding consideration. They are convinced that participation does not imply

## The Dilemma of Diversity and Unity

recognition of the religious legitimacy or authority of the Reform and Conservative movements.

There may well be other reasons for the firm position taken by the modern-liberal orthodox camp on this issue. To leave these powerful established councils and boards would mean depriving themselves from many benefits derived through belonging, such as chaplaincies, media exposure and access to high government circles. Another reason, though rarely articulated, is their belief that accepting the Issur and bowing to the incessant demands of the traditional camp to withdraw from mixed rabbinic and synagogue groups would be interpreted as their capitulation to the yeshiva world and 'right wing'. This could hardly be tolerated since it would be a victory for the militants and a defeat for the moderates.

The camp within orthodoxy which favors withdrawal from these organizations builds its case on a number of persuasive arguments. First and foremost is the question of granting legitimacy to the concept of denominations in Judaism. The traditionalists are convinced that joint participation of rabbis and laymen in organizations that are clearly identified as rabbinic or congregational in name and spirit must perforce imply recognition of equally acceptable authentic religious expressions within Judaism. Orthodox participation in umbrella groups gives the impression to Jew and non-Jew alike that all rabbis are Torah scholars and committed to *Halacha*, hence their authority and decision making power is equal. That all houses of worship are holy, hence permissible for even observant Jews to frequent and that all marriages, divorces and conversions are valid regardless of one's adherence to Jewish law and practice as established in the *Shulchan Aruch*.

The emergence in recent years of spiritual leaders who deny not only the divine origin of Torah and the permanence of Jewish law, but the Divinity itself, serves to strengthen their implacable opposition in fostering this misconception of equality by calling men who are guilty of transgressing the most fundamental laws of Torah rabbis and teachers of Judaism! In recent years even the New York Board of Rabbis has refused to accept as members clergymen who officiate at mixed marriages although they are still tolerant of those members who violate the Shabbos, kashruth and reject the fundamental Jewish laws regarding marriage, divorce and conver-

## The Dilemma of Diversity and Unity

sion. It is therefore understandable that there are orthodox rabbis who *refuse* to belong to the Board of Rabbis although *in favor* of continued orthodox participation in the Synagogue Council of America, which at least does not present itself as an organization of Jewish teachers and spiritual leaders but rather as a purely congregational and community body.

Another reason for the traditional forces' opposition to membership in umbrella organizations is that the myth of denominations in Judaism, demeans orthodoxy, reducing the historic authentic voice of Torah to one of three 'legitimate' expressions of the Jewish faith. Finally, the most important reason of all is that this camp within orthodoxy has the highest regard for the *daas* Torah (Torah opinion) of those outstanding Roshei Yeshiva who issued the Issur twenty years ago and therefore are adamant in their position, motivated by a disciplined adherence to any Halachic decision emanating from such illustrious teachers of Torah.

The anti-S.C.A. forces reject the recent argument made by the current orthodox President of the S.C.A., who stated that orthodoxy is now strong enough to meet with Reform and Conservative spokesmen without fear, hence there is no excuse according to his reasoning for them to continue to boycott the Synagogue Council of America or similar intra-religious groups. The traditional camp considers this a complete misrepresentation of their position since they have never been motivated by fear of contamination or dilution. The question was always simply one of refusal to join with such groups, convinced that this would grant tacit recognition to their legitimacy. It is interesting to note that in the initial stages of this debate the pro-S.C.A. camp preached unity and *ahavas Yisroel*, accusing the other camp of being separatists and woefully lacking in love of their fellow Jews. This argument has been effectively refuted in the past number of years and now a new argument is projected, namely the fear of contamination which, they now argue, has been reduced since orthodoxy has built up its resistance. It seems ironic to many observers that those who for years participated in umbrella groups out of weakness and a sense of inferiority now demand that others join them out of strength and a sense of superiority! It should be made clear that the traditional camp does not oppose participation and involvement in Jewish organizations who are concerned with Jewish civil rights, the security of the State of Israel or the problem of Russian Jewry, since these bodies do not present themselves as expressions of Jewish *religious* ideology but rather as organized bodies of k'lal Yisroel concerned for the welfare of their fellow Jews.

For many years a number of rabbinic groups, the U.O.J.C.A., Agudath Israel and certain elements in the yeshiva world have called for the establishment of an Orthodox Council incorporating all national orthodox groups which they feel would present a clear image and project an eloquent voice of Torah on the American scene. A united vigorous force such as this would have vibrancy and strength which a divided orthodox community lacks and would make an impact upon the American Jewish community at large. This idea of an Orthodox Council is subscribed to by both camps in orthodoxy.

Certain halting steps have been taken from time to time to bring about the formation of this Council but there are many obstacles, not the least of which is the unfortunate climate of suspicion and distrust which prevails within the orthodox community. One cannot ignore the tension between the right wing and the center, between the yeshiva oriented world and the synagogue-rabbinical world. Time has proven that there is a large grouping within the modern rabbinate that suffers from a strange ambivalence, a sense of superiority on the one hand coupled with a sense of inadequacy and concern regarding their non-acceptance by the Torah world. One must face up to the reality of the synagogue world's vulnerability due to their weak synagogue standards and bending of the halacha on many occasions. This in turn evokes an attitude of *bitul* on the part of the yeshiva world countered by aggressive reaction on the part of the synagogue leaders. In such a climate the creation of a viable meaningful Council is indeed quite difficult. In all frankness, the heavy-handed tactics of the right are, at times, also quite distasteful. Their inability to appreciate the daily problems confronting the orthodox rabbinical and synagogue leadership in smaller Jewish communities contributes to this tension.

The greatest obstacle, however, is still the continued membership of the Rabbinical Council of America and the U.O.J.C.A. in the Synagogue Council, which to the right wing, is an insurmountable one. To them withdrawal is an a priori condition while the liberal

## The Dilemma of Diversity and Unity

camp argues that first a new home must be established before asking them to leave the Synagogue Council lest they be homeless until an Orthodox Council is firmly entrenched. The question, therefore, that must be answered by each group is, what price are they willing to pay to establish orthodox unity? The pro-Synagogue Council group must be willing to pay the price of forgoing its relationship with the heterodox in return for the friendship of their Torah committed brethren while the anti-Synagogue Council forces must be willing to pay the price of patience, good faith and good will by uniting with all Torah forces without setting pre-conditions. Unfortunately, a stalemate presently exists with mutual distrust increasing and the chasm widening. There are many in both camps who believe that unless orthodox leaders are willing to pay the price for unity the cost will be far greater, namely the continued fragmentation of the orthodox in the United States.

At the end of Tractate 'Edyos' Rabbi Yehuda is of the opinion that Elijah will come before the advent of the *Moshiach* for the purpose, "to bring close, not to divide"—*l'karev aval lo l'rachak*. Although he is referring to a question of family purity and lineage, this statement homiletically has been interpreted in the following intriguing manner. The Hebrew word for truth is *'emet'*, comprised of three letters, separated by the total spectrum of the Hebrew alphabet—an *'aleph'* and *'taf'*, the first and last letters with a *'mem'* in the center—the middle-most letter of the alphabet. The Hebrew word for falsehood is *'sheker'*, composed of three letters that are next to each other in the alphabet, *'shin'*, *'kaf'* and *'resh'*. This strange variance implies that the forces of 'sheker', who distort Judaism are usually united, whereas those who champion authentic Yiddishkeit are hopelessly divided. Now, there are two solutions to this problem. One is to divide and thereby conquer the forces of 'sheker' the other is to unify the camps of Torah. Which of these will Elijah choose? Rabbi Yehuda is of the firm opinion that the solution is not *l'rachek*, to separate the close knit ranks of 'sheker' and disrupt the united front of the heterodox camp, but rather *l'karev* to bring together the 'aleph', 'mem' and 'taf' of "emet", the various factions within the camp of Torah-true Jewry.

The imperative of the future commands the United States orthodox community to channel its strength a little less in combating the non and anti-Torah forces and far more in exerting its energy and will toward the goal of unity within its own Torah ranks.

\*   \*   \*

We have attempted to present in these opening chapters a picture of American Orthodoxy, an analysis of its strengths and shortcomings, the areas of dissension and the problems of disunity which confront it at the present time. In spite of all these shortcomings and vexing problems, orthodoxy is experiencing a resurgence both in the United States and Israel. The source of its strength is drawn from three reservoirs — the home, the school and the shul. These three forces contribute to the stability and growth of Torah Jewry but there are tensions here as well: between day school and home, the Rav and the Rosh Yeshiva, the yeshiva graduate and the shul. The following chapters will address themselves to these topics.

## Chapter 4

# Day Schools, Yeshivoth, and the Community

Much has been said of the effect, the impact, and at times the revolutionary influence of the day school upon the home and family. The obvious has not been permitted, in this case, to escape us. Our responsibility is — in all honesty and frankness, and with a great deal of integrity — to examine the lasting effects after removing a bit of the veneer which would have peeled regardless. We must ask ourselves: Wherein can we improve and strengthen the influence of school upon home? We must carefully examine the inter-relationship between school and home.

The areas we shall analyze and discuss — will be the following:
1) Religious observance in the home and by the family as a unit outside the home;
2) Parent education: the degree of Jewish knowledge, and increased interest and pursuit of Torah study by yeshiva parents;
3) The relationship between home and school; faculty and parents;
4) The entire question of "values." Are Torah-values being transmitted in the home, or is the school being delegated to do the job of parents — in such areas as: ethics, morality, *derech eretz* (simple basic respect) and *tzenius* (modesty).

These latter areas are those which belong to the home far more so than to the teacher. And yet, how much is being given in the home? Iss the Yeshiva curriculum geared to teach these values and transmit standards, so that the child will be able to bring them into the home and perhaps irritate the mind of the parent and imbue the heart of the parent with a certain spirit so that these values can ultimately be transmitted from parent to child.

5) The plaguing, frustrating question of continuity and permanence. What and how much will remain? What person who has worked for a yeshiva hasn't asked himself that question; what teacher hasn't asked himself that question; and what parent hasn't asked himself that question? How much will remain 10 years from now, 15 years from now, 20 years from now? What effect, ultimately, will these children, who are being trained by us, have upon the community?

Once the pupil has left the day school, the home will then have to play the almost exclusive role — combining the heretofore divided roles of school and home — of guarding Torah ideals and practices. Now the question is: Is the home equipped; is the home ready — can it guard the Torah ideals and principles? Are the parents properly equipped or do they have the *will* to conserve and not dissipate what has already been won in the day school years?

These are the problems. These are real problems that we cannot escape. And we must, above all, not allow ourselves to be misled into thinking that we have already solved our problems; that once a day school enters a community, we have saved the future for Judaism in that community. We must realize that in education improvement is always possible, while, somehow, perfection is always denied.

Admittedly — and I am sure that you have heard such reports from all over the country — there are homes and families who have been changed for the better as a result of day school pupils and the exposure of parents to the school. We would ask, however, whether the changing of dishes in various homes has been matched equally by the changing of *shul* affiliation? Has the change in the way of life wrought by the day school also been matched by a change in attitude, in the concepts and values of what *Yiddishkeit* really means. Does the commitment to *Shabbos* and *kashrus* carry forth beyond the home, as well, and beyond the period of school attendance. In brief, are we not being pleasantly deluded by shallow, superficial, symbolic observance, without deep, sincere, lasting commitment — reflecting perhaps a weakness in the modern day school structure, where depth has been sacrificed for width, quality for quantity, and an obsession for statistics has resulted in shallowness.

Adult education, as it is understood in our present society (as distinguished from Torah study groups in *Chumash, Mishnah* and

## Day Schools, Yeshivoth, and the Community

Talmud in the traditional *beth-hamedrash* milieu), will at best whet the appetite and at worst satisfy it. Probably the norm is to be found somewheres between these two poles. The unlettered parent will as soon develop a sense of frustration and even resentment at his or her child's mastery of the mysterious as he or she will be prodded and propelled into keeping up with David's or Miriam's pace of progress. A well thought-out program, with a sense of continuity and growth, must be developed by the school and synagogue working together, if the latter is to be exploited properly. The day school child can indeed be an irritant, intellectually speaking, in the home — but wisdom and judgment are required so that the irritant be positively and properly channelled.

The school can but teach, the home must translate into action. The school, if you will, preaches — the home must practice. The teacher can instruct, the parent must implement. Inspiration of course comes from both; but the fires must be fed not dampened — and the home fires must be kept burning. Conflicts between what is taught in the school and what is practiced at home are as ancient as that moment in history when the lofty concepts and philosophies of the academic halls became inimicable with the cruel demands of a market-place mentality and a success-intoxicated society. How much more so is this true when the religious teachings of the yeshiva classroom have a head-on collision with a secular-oriented home. Of course, one can take the convenient attitude (quite prevalent in the highest circles in recent years) that the way to cope with grave problems is through massive unconcern, in the hope that by ignoring their existence they will go away. This we reject. We also reject the strange casting of the school in the role of transmitter of *norms*, namely: "ethnic" culture, symbols of identifications, and perhaps even "religion" — while the home remains, at best, neutral.

We do submit that the school has every right to expect full cooperation of the parents and home in avoiding the conflicts and inconsistencies which have plagued us for so long. When parents are convinced of the sincerity and pure motivation of the school — and realize the impossibility of compromise on the school's part — then if something has "to give," it will perforce be the parent!

Ideally, home and school complement one another. Separate, distinct areas of training the child are not clearly defined; nor are there lines of demarcation — as such. We do feel, however, that knowledge and skills somehow belong to the school domain while development of character, values, standards, and *middos* cannot ultimately be delegated to the teacher — but must emanate from the parent. We are faced today, to a great degree, with convenient delegation and irresponsible abdication on the part of parents. Too many parents — yeshiva parents — are guilty of abandoning the traditional role of shaping and molding the ethical and moral character of their children. They are not fostering attitudes, values and standards which children must absorb in the home more so than they can in the school.

*Derech eretz* can be strengthened in the classroom; it must, however, originate in the home. *Tzenius* can be taught in the Yeshiva; it must be practiced, however, in the home. A sense of duty and responsibility can be cultivated in the school; it must be observed, however, in parents, by their children — in the home and in the community. The ethical will and moral choice are virtues and powers which cannot be committed to memory nor learnt by rote — these must be developed. This can be done only by gearing our curriculum more intensively towards this goal and educating parents that they must resume their place on the seat of authority and responsibility. The sad combination of absentee-fathers, self-centered mothers, child-centered homes and a secular-materialistic centered society cries out for an intensification in the school curriculum of Torah-oriented, ethical, moral and "value concepts," coupled with a concerted, compelling call to parents to be precisely that — parents!

In an adult-oriented culture — in other words, in the traditional society — the child is *prepared* for adulthood. In a child-centered society, it is difficult to ascertain just what the child is being prepared for — unless it be to have children so that the cycle can be started again as rapidly as possible. In the area of Jewish "religion" and "education" — in today's average community — we indeed find an almost exclusive emphasis placed upon the minors. As soon as one reaches his majority (i.e. bar-mitzvah), he is at a terminal point. He is now an adult and as such is no longer obligated to conform since he is now confirmed. He has reached the enviable state of irresponsible maturity. Now, to what extent is this true of the day school student? What degree of piety, knowledge and commitment to Torah will he carry forth with him?

## Day Schools, Yeshivoth, and the Community

I submit that — as presently constituted — it is doubtful whether our curriculum is coming to grips realistically with the obvious truth that large numbers of *pupils* terminate their studies at the threshold of high school — as they enter into their teens, certainly the most crucial period in the development of the individual. What is being done to inculcate them with some depth of piety and devotion to Torah which shall not be lost in a brief period of time? Should we not stress, more and more, reverence, worship, observance, piety, *mussar* — so that if not a great scholar one shall at least remain a Torah-Jew!

We must bend every effort towards insuring the retention of an attitude, an acceptance, an appreciation and, G-d willing, an appetite — for more! We must give the pupil guide-lines, directions, which will lead him toward identification with the Torah community; the orthodox synagogue, the orthodox Rabbi, and the various institutions of orthodoxy. Otherwise, we may find ourselves preparing excellent material for the deviationist camp. The day school must vigorously and boldly align itself unequivocally with those forces in the community where its administration would hope to see their students active ten years and twenty years hence. This, unfortunately, has not always been the case — for public relations, monetary or other reasons unbeknown to the naive observer. In summation, it would be the height of tragedy to ever witness what has been built by orthodox money, tears, dreams, and sweat inherited by those elements who would dilute and destroy all we hold precious and sacred. We have accomplished much in the past two decades with G-d's help. We have stemmed the tide of reform, battled the dragon of *am-ha'aratzus* (ignorance), made the word yeshiva fashionable; but it is not enough to endure — we must also prevail. To do so, we must honestly and fearlessly face up to our shortcomings — as well as accept praise for our achievements. Opportunity is still ours, ever knocking — for opportunity knocks as often as a man has an ear trained to hear it, an eye to see it, a hand trained to grasp it. We realize that many are the obstacles which lie in the path of perfection, and many of our suggestions will be difficult to implement. So it must be. The indelicate hand of necessity is forever leaving its fingerprints on the fragile crystal of our dreams. But dream we must!

We cannot afford to rest on our laurels — for the times are frantic and threaten to pass us by, unless we move vigorously, courageously and swiftly. The work is yet great — let not the laborers be lethargic. Not good intentions — but good, dramatic deeds will pave the road to our victory.

# Chapter 5

# The Rabbi and the Rosh Yeshiva

Scholars and sages have played a crucial leadership role throughout our history. The bearers and teachers of Torah selflessly dedicated themselves to attain the fulfillment and realization of the Jewish people's mission, guarding zealously the source of Israel's true strength — the knowledge, pursuit, and practice of Torah. For the past two thousand years in particular, bereft of king, priest, or prophet, it is obvious that we owe our continued existence as a people, our internal unity and discipline, our common experience and goals, to rabbinic, Torah-scholar leadership.

For many centuries the areas in which the Torah leader functioned — whether known as *rav*, *marbitz Torah*, or *chacham* — were varied and broad in scope. He was teacher and preacher, community leader and judge, statesman and author of responsa. The position and power of the *morah de'asroh* were neither uniform nor equal at all times, or in all localities. Nevertheless, it is apparent to us that, in general, the rabbi commanded respect and obedience, and wielded great influence over his community.

The records and sources concerning the rabbinate during the 18th and 19th centuries indicate that the rabbi's duties were great, and so were his honors, rewards, and prestige. His primary duty was to establish and conduct a yeshiva which the community agreed to support; it was the common practice that the rav was also the *rosh mesivta*.

The role of the rabbi as *marbitz Torah*, disseminator of Torah, is especially apparent in Sephardic communities. As early as the *Takanos* of 1432, the primary stress is placed on the duty of the rabbi — indeed reflected by the title of rabbi — to disseminate Torah, in addition to his function as judge and arbiter of controversies and civil cases.

In time, as communities grew and the rabbi's functions and duties increased, a rosh yeshiva was retained, by the rav, to help relieve him of this taxing role, although he still continued to give *shiurim* in the yeshiva. It is interesting to note that in Mir, where one of the great yeshivos of modern days was established in 1815, the rav and rosh yeshiva were one and the same, and even when a rosh yeshiva was retained the rav continued his active role until a conflict arose in 1867 between the rabbi and the rosh yeshiva. The rav complained that he was not invited to give shiurim in the yeshiva or participate in its administration. The case was submitted to a Beis Din (among others, those who sat on the court were: Rabbi Isaac Elchanan Spektor, Reb Eisel Charif of Slonim and the Warsaw Rav, Dov-Beresh Meislis) and the decision was in favor of the rosh yeshiva. It was felt that these two areas — the rabbinical and the yeshiva-educational — were separate and distinct. Although in later years the rav of Mir did serve as second rosh yeshiva, this was due in every instance to some family connection. The story of Mir is not unusual or unique — it is rather indicative of a new development and evolutionary process which took place during the past hundred years or so. The roles of community rabbi and rosh yeshiva grew to be quite separate and distinct, even though never defined formally: the rabbi served as 'master of the city,' concerned with its every religious and spiritual need and fulfilling all rabbinic functions — while the rosh yeshiva emerged as the head of the Torah academy, educator, and quite often author of scholarly writings, but rarely of responsa, for that belonged to the realm of the rabbi.

During the early years of Jewish religious life in the United States, the European pattern was followed quite closely — the role of the rabbi and the position of the synagogue was all-important. Rabbis played prominent roles not only in purely religious affairs but also in the areas of philanthropy, politics, and social services. But there was one exception to the European pattern: the yeshivos were yet to appear. True, the Talmud Torah in many communities was on a par with some contemporary day schools, but the yeshiva gedolah was unknown, and of course the rosh yeshiva was not, as yet, a member of Jewish leadership. When yeshivoth, eventually were founded, the rosh yeshiva confined himself to his natural area of activity — the educational one. Thus, the administration of the

## The Rabbi and the Rosh Yeshiva

Agudas Harabonim was vested in the hands of rabbis of communities and synagogues, who lived, breathed, and practiced *rabbonus*.

Today — reflecting the radical change that has occurred in the Torah community — the majority of the presidium of the Agudas Harabonim consists of roshei yeshivos and *not* rabbis of synagogues. The incursion of the rosh yeshiva into the traditional domain of the rabbi is obvious. The rosh yeshiva is more likely to be the *mesader kiddushin* at a wedding, than the rabbi of the bride or groom. Halachic questions are directed to the rosh yeshiva by individuals and communities, rather than to *rabbonim*. This occurs unhappily even in cases where the community leadership has already posed the question to their rabbi and then goes over his head to verify his ruling with a rosh yeshiva. Even the time-honored title of Rav has been transferred from the synagogue or community rabbi and is granted only to the rosh yeshiva, although the rabbi may be an outstanding Torah scholar and the rosh yeshiva only an instructor in Talmud.

What has caused this downgrading of the rabbi and why has the rosh yeshiva entered into the field of rabbinical activity? What effect is this having upon the *kehillah* and the entire institution of rabbonus? Above all, how is this disruption in the respective roles of rabbi and rosh yeshiva affecting the strength, position, and future of the Torah community in the U.S.A.? These are some pertinent questions we should address ourselves to, in a search for answers that are vital to our Torah future.

The destruction of the great European Torah centers resulted in the transfer of certain yeshivos to these shores and marked the arrival of a number of great roshei yeshiva who aroused renewed devotion to Torah study, on a higher level than had been pursued heretofore in America. A new type of *bnei* Torah was developed over the years, imbued with the special values and standards of bnei yeshiva. Many became educators, some rabbonim, and many more businessmen. Few, unfortunately, became shul *baalebatim*. The average ben yeshiva has little use for the community synagogue and the rabbi is varyingly ignored, pitied, tolerated, or reluctantly recognized.

This attitude has been fostered, although at times unintentionally, by the spirit prevailing in the yeshivoth. The yeshiva world maintains that the tempo of the times, the demands of the modern

## The Rabbi and the Rosh Yeshiva

day synagogue, the low caliber of the average shul member, all conspire to transform the rabbi into an executive and social director, a minister and preacher — but not a *lamdon* or *moreh horo'oh*. There is much truth to this thesis, but little effort is made to recognize the reasons and find a solution.

At the heart of this vexing problem which has sapped the vitality and health of the Torah community in our country, lies a deceptively simple but tragically overlooked fact. To be a mature, learned, real rav, one needs mature, learned, real baalebatim. No rabbi has ever come forth from the yeshiva fully developed. He grew and matured — developed in stature and learning — because his people asked *she'elos*, attended his shiurim, respected his Torah wisdom and guidance. If those who have the qualifications to be such baalebatim, refuse to play this role and abdicate their responsibilities, thereby abandoning the rabbi to laymen unversed in Torah, then they insure the diminution of the rabbi in his Torah knowledge and practically preclude any opportunity for his growth and development. With the resultant decline of rabbonus, bnei Torah have turned to the roshei yeshiva, transforming them in effect into rabbis. Many of the roshei yeshiva have not sought this role, nor do they welcome it; but unfortunately, instead of training the bulk of their pupils to become responsible congregants, so that their superior disciples can become real rabbonim, they are doing very little to resolve the dilemma.

What is the harm in this situation? In the first place, many a rosh yeshiva, while an outstanding lamdon, is not an experienced moreh horo'oh — while the community rabbi, if given the opportunity to function in this field which is his, can and should develop into a competent halachic authority. This competence can only be fostered if the *kovod harabbonus* is nurtured by the bnei yeshiva, and they will agree to deprive themselves of their comfortable dependence upon their rosh yeshiva, relying instead upon the skill and sincere search for Torah truth of the rav.

The diminution of kovod harabbonus has also had harmful effects in the field of Jewish education. The Orthodox rav, when transformed into a rabbi, is put on a par with Conservative and Reform clergy. Now, the paramount importance of the day school in American Jewish life is no longer ignored by the deviationist forces, and they seek a role in these schools. As a result — faced with the need to establish a clear policy — day school administrators have been led either to *include* all rabbis, or to *exclude* them all. The role of the Orthodox rabbi as molder of the Torah image in the community is one that cannot be fulfilled unless he is involved in the chinuch of his community. When this role is denied him, or no distinction is made between his role and that of the deviationist clergyman, a bitter harvest is bound to be harvested in but a few brief years.

Also, lines of demarcation between the pulpit rabbi and the businessman rabbi have been erased. Strangely, in many instances, the businessman rabbi has taken over day school leadership, while community rabbis have been removed from positions of influence. This development ignores the fact that the practicing rabbi, whatever his failings, still retains that special Torah approach which is a natural consequence of his professional position.

As a result of the denigration of rabbonus in our time we are confronted with qualitative depreciation in the ranks of rabbinical candidates. The rabbinate has always presented a great challenge, even though a difficult calling — "the worst of all trades but the best of all professions," as one perceptive observer put it. Today, however, every yeshiva is confronted with the problem of their best students refusing to enter the rabbinate, while the less able student who cannot foresee a successful career in mathematics or physics chooses the rabbinate as a safe, soft status profession. In some yeshivos the students eschew these technical fields of endeavor to continue their Torah studies at a *kollel*, leading to a career in the field of chinuch. Their goal is to attain the coveted title of "rosh yeshiva" — even if in practice they only teach a class of beginner's Talmud.

Whatever the motivations, one inescapable fact confronts us: we are not producing the rabbinical leadership which our Torah communities will need in the next decade. This can only be rectified by elevating the kovod harabonus, which can only be achieved by the yeshivos urging their best students to enter the rabbinate, while encouraging all their *talmidim* who will not become rabbonim to become baalebatim.

The weakness apparent so often in the Torah community is not due to our lack of numbers or power as such, but to our failure to mobilize our forces and the splintering of the power we do possess.

To change this situation, a two-way street must be opened. The rabbi and the synagogue must support fully the yeshiva and its leadership, while the yeshiva heads must speak out forthrightly in behalf of the rabbinate and the synagogue. In this way the existing tension between the two worlds will be eased, and the prestige and power of Torah will be enhanced.

## Chapter 6

# The Yeshiva Alumnus and the Synagogue

For lo these many years we have been told from pulpit, platform, and by the printed word that the yeshiva-trained layman, be he businessman, professional, or artisan, would some day transform the face of the Jewish community. The fruits of the yeshivoth would bring an infusion of new blood into the anemic, weakened arteries of traditional Judaism's institutions and organizations. To a certain extent this optimistic vision and prophecy has been fulfilled. There is today a vibrancy, a vitality, and a sense of fresh energy to be found in the orthodox Jewish communal structure. We are indeed beginning to reap the harvest of a few decades of yeshiva plantings.

Concomitant with this welcome and heartening trend some serious stocktaking is in order — a little *cheshbon hanefesh*. Let us ask some pertinent and challenging questions. What is the relationship of the yeshiva-oriented and trained *baal-habayis* to the community synagogue? To what extent is his presence felt in the school? What impact has he made on community projects which are an integral part and by-product of the *shul*? What unique role, if any, does he play in the synagogue? In what manner is the rabbi, together with the synagogue membership, affected by the appearance of this new species on the American Jewish scene?

A careful study of various communities where a concentration of yeshiva alumni is found will reveal some strange and startling facts. True, a goodly number of yeshiva-trained laymen, among them some former practicing rabbis, are congregants of synagogues and *do* take an active part in community affairs. A sizeable group, however, carefully avoid the synagogue and are conspicuous by their absence in many areas of community endeavor. They establish smaller private *minyonim* or patronize a local *shtibel*. They avoid the synagogue, both as congregants and participants, though it should be noted that many are members in name only for reasons best known to themselves and/or the energetic membership chairman of the local synagogue. This abstention of yeshiva graduates from the synagogue results in a two-fold puzzlement.

One confused individual is the "simple" *baal-habayis* who cannot understand why the learned and pious young family man who lives down the street has isolated himself from the mainstream of the community and its heart — the synagogue. He finds it difficult to comprehend this resistance to becoming an active member of the wider Jewish community. Indeed, he wonders why this individual does not assume a role of leadership considering his Torah knowledge, standard of observance, and spirit of piety.

The other perplexed person is the very subject of this puzzlement, namely the yeshiva-trained layman. This nice "yunger man" cannot understand why he *should* affiliate himself with a community synagogue. In many cases a synagogue is not part of his background and he is frankly ill at ease within its walls. This is due to the fact that during his youth he patronized either a shtibel or *davened* in the beth hamidrash of his alma mater.

He is nonplussed at the occasional admonition leveled by rabbi or lay leader, which he feels is an invasion of his privacy and freedom of choice. These demands, that he become a congregant, threaten to disrupt his comfortable little world; convenient minyon, little coterie of *limud Torah chaverim*, and a cozy state of detachment.

Let us, therefore, address ourselves to both parties to this dilemma. Let us attempt to analyze the motivations, conscious and otherwise, of the yeshiva alumnus resulting in this strange behavior of isolation. Let us also explain the reasons for the deep disappointment and frustration felt by rabbis and synagogue leaders as a result of this detachment and noninvolvement.

When a young man who has lived many years in a yeshiva environment moves into the newer city neighborhood or suburbia, he brings with him views and attitudes molded and fostered in that milieu. Among them is a certain *bitul*, a belittlement and disparagement of the modern manifestations of the American Jewish community. A major target of this attitude is the synagogue-center. The evolution of the modern shul into a social center, with religious activity shunted to the periphery, is an image firmly

## The Yeshiva Alumnus and the Synagogue

embedded in the mind-eye of the yeshiva student. His negative, almost antagonistic attitude borders on contempt, coupled with a determination to escape this distasteful communal affiliation and identification. This image is not dispelled, alas, in most cases and the alumnus, strengthened in his preconceived prejudices, shuns the shul and strikes his community roots elsewhere.

He would be pained and shocked if one would intimate that his point of view is one that could be termed "peace unto my soul and a plague on all your houses." It is so, nonetheless. Secession may grant him comfort and a cozy sense of superiority but it creates more problems than it solves. Above all it is a shattering of the fond dream entertained for years by responsible Jewish leaders; namely that some day the yeshiva-trained layman would revolutionize our synagogues and change the face of our communities; within, not without, the framework of the synagogue.

In addition to the antipathy engendered in some yeshivoth toward the modern synagogue, regardless of its traditional structure and spirit, there is a characteristic of the yeshiva alumnus which serves as an added barrier between himself and orientation to a shul. This implanted yeshiva trait is an impatience with pomp and ceremony, formality, and ritual. One who has participated in a so-called "yeshiva-davening" for many years in the beth-hamidrosh finds the average synagogue services quite uncomfortable. This service, with its attendant congregational singing, sermon, lengthy Torah reading and insistence upon decorum, to name but a few encumbrances, is distasteful and tedious to the yeshiva-trained worshipper.

There are other motivations which are perhaps not as apparent or discernible, nor are they, in all candidness, usually admitted or expressed. There may well be an understandable reluctance to do so. The *talmid chochom*, American style, finds it a mite unpleasant to be part of the mass, to be submerged and thereby lose his unique identity. He is disinclined to become indistinguishable from other members of the community.

This is, indeed, a form of intellectual snobbery, stemming from a sense of religious and academic superiority. Nonetheless, it is quite understandable and should be commiserated with rather than condemned. The yeshiva alumnus hungers for a degree of recognition. If a niche can be found for his talents he will usually emerge from his glorious isolation to receive this recognition and honor.

One should also mention in this connection an inherent unwillingness to accept the prosaic role of *baal-habayis*, for it is somehow difficult for him to accept authority and discipline. It is paradoxical that the person who gladly accepts the authority and discipline of Torah finds it so difficult to accept the disciplines of society and the community. Since this discipline is perforce mandatory in any reputable, responsible synagogue, it becomes a difficult obstacle, in the path of the yeshiva-trained layman, to overcome and surmount. Maturity is desperately needed to accept the role and rule of rabbi and lay leadership. Unfortunately, maturity is a rare attribute in today's world.

The yeshiva bochur (incidentally, a properly chosen appellation if one accepts the concept of "you can take the bochur out of the yeshiva, but you can't take the yeshiva out of the bochur") often laments that he has infrequent opportunity for Torah study since his departure from the beth-midrash walls. There is so little free time to learn due to the insistent demands of *parnosah*. We therefore find that a major reason presented for davening with a quick, small minyon (short-order style) is to grant one a few additional precious Shabboth hours for *limud Torah*. In all fairness there are quite a number who *do* utilize this found time for the noble purpose of Torah study.

The embarrassing fact, which in quite a number of other cases transforms this seemingly valid reason into a weak excuse, is the convivial weekly "home and home" *kiddush* schedule. This phenomenon, which unfortunately is not rare, finds our scholar arriving home at a later hour than would be the case had he attended the synagogue with its lengthy services.

One final objection to synagogue participation, often heard, is that most synagogues are run by a few rich men which would place the sincere, observant layman in the untenable position of fighting a lonely, hopeless battle against these vested interests. The reasoning is that if he would attempt to introduce his unique high standards into the shul he would be in the unenviable position of being outnumbered, outweighed, and outvoted. Is it not true, the argument goes, that the majority of synagogue members are not really interested in changing the mediocrity of standards and values

## The Yeshiva Alumnus and the Synagogue

as manifested in the synagogue of today? The secular, banal activity of Men's Club, Sisterhood, and Couples Club will not allow itself to be replaced by Torah study, cultural activities, and strengthening of authentic Jewish practices within the synagogue-center. The needs of the elite few will be engulfed in the wants of the many.

Although these are strong and valid objections, they do not justify, in our opinion, the rejection of the synagogue with the resultant establishment of splinter groups.

The yeshiva alumnus should consider the possibility that in his abject surrender to the "inevitable" triumph of the mediocrity of the many and vested power of the few, he has made no real, concerted effort to revolutionize the modern orthodox synagogue. This should be his special responsibility, a challenge to be faced, not avoided. It is often true in a shul, as it is in the political area, that if a voter is not counted it is not necessarily due to the fact that he is denied the vote, but simply because he has failed to register. He may well have disenfranchised himself!

In all affiliation one must realize that it is not the solemn assignment of rights and duties but the seizing of opportunities which result in the greatest victories. This is no less true in a synagogue than it is in any organized group. That today's synagogues are rife with golden opportunities awaiting an elite, knowledgeable, dedicated, committed group, none will deny — unless he has refused to acquaint himself with the elementary facts of contemporary Jewish community life. It is difficult at times not to conclude that some of our fine religious Jews are innocent of what really is transpiring in the synagogue world. The image they have created is oft a very beclouded one, resulting from lack of close observation and involvement. Distance may well dim perspective; it should not be permitted to distort it.

We have addressed ourselves to the motivation, admitted or otherwise, prompting the yeshiva alumnus in his negative attitude toward the community synagogue. Let us now present the case for the synagogue. Why is the shul so important and why should the yeshiva graduate be congregant, member, participant, and leader?

With the destruction of the Temple and dispersion of the Jews, the *Beth Hak'nesseth* became the miniature sanctuary. For thousands of years the shul has been the center, the *merkaz*, the hub around which revolves all community activity. From it emanates all positive

## The Yeshiva Alumnus and the Synagogue

Jewish endeavor. It is the second home of the religious Jew; his meeting place, government house, club house, and study hall, all concentrated in one structure. In modern times the synagogue is still that vehicle which can best initiate, execute, and implement all positive projects. *Chinuch, tzedokah, kashruth, mikvah*, these are all channeled through a united *kehillah* functioning through the synagogue.

Much criticism has been leveled lately against the modern synagogue-center for relegating its authentic Jewish activity to an insignificant corner, while the social, athletic, and quasi-cultural projects are granted priority and enjoy far greater popularity. This, unfortunately, is true in many cases. This sad state of affairs will be corrected, we submit, only if a group of intelligent, Jewishly-committed young men and women are prepared to make their voice heard and their presence felt. This is the first and foremost challenge which confronts our yeshiva products. Many have fortunately risen to the challenge and successfully transformed the synagogue into a miniature sanctuary. Many more, alas, have unfortunately evaded their responsibility to the detriment of k'lal Yisroel.

The presence of this elite element lends dignity and stature to a synagogue, though not in the usual, accepted sense of the word. In the past, the affluence and social position of a synagogue's membership set the tone and determined the status of that institution in the community. Today, however, we have the unique opportunity of establishing a new kind of prestige through the medium of the Jewish calibre and quality of a synagogue's membership. Observant, learned, American-reared orthodox Jewish men and women bring to a synagogue a unique character which cannot be duplicated by other "denominations" in Jewish life. Our brethren in the deviationist camps can certainly surpass us when the yardstick used is that of wealth and social position. They cannot hope to compete with us, in terms of prestige, if we can present to the world a picture of synagogues comprised of dedicated, committed, and loyally observant Jewish families. Therein lies our greatest strength. How heart-breaking, therefore, to witness this strength dissipated through fragmentation and splintering. Only when united in the synagogue can this force be felt, heard, and respected by the entire community.

The mediocre standards of the modern synagogue, this source of great lamentation and criticism, could be elevated through the transfusion of yeshiva-trained laymen. Their affiliation would emphatically enhance the dignity and set the tone for the synagogue. Let us even be so bold as to submit that the rabbi would also grow in Torah and *chochmah* if he had to meet the constant challenge of a Jewishly intelligent, learned congregation. Too often does the promising intellect and fresh thinking of the young rabbi become atrophied, prematurely stale, and trite due to the lack of challenge from his congregants.

Apropos of this thought, let us submit an argument which may not be too readily appreciated by the yeshiva-trained layman. I refer to the example which he sets for others in the congregation. The average layman looks to the learned element for his cue in determining his degree of *derech eretz* to shul and rabbi. If this *derech eretz* is forthcoming from the elite element it has its beneficial effects upon the congregation as a whole. Conversely, when the yeshiva alumnus is indifferent or at times even discourteous to the spiritual leadership of the synagogue he must accept the onus of diminishing the respect of others who look to him for guidance.

The hands of the rabbi would certainly be greatly strengthened in guarding the pristine traditional character of the shul if there were but a nucleus of strongly committed and articulate orthodox laymen in the congregation. How often it comes to pass that the religious elements chastise and censure the rabbi for allowing certain questionable practices and innovations to be introduced into the synagogue. How tragic that these same pious, sincere individuals were not present or sufficiently interested to be involved at the moment of battle when these policies were introduced. It is far more important to participate in the righteous struggle than to strike a pose of self-righteousness after the battle has been lost.

What is so often overlooked by yeshiva graduates is the effect of their detachment upon their own children. What attitude toward kehillah, rav, communal responsibility, and unity is fostered when children are withdrawn from the main stream of the Jewish community in which they live? Certainly this is an integral part of chinuch, on a par with formal academic education. The self-sufficiency, real or imagined, which is the "blessing" of the father may not adequately be visited upon the sons. By this we mean, what guarantee is there that those of the next generation will be properly trained to take their places in the Jewish community of their choice, once they leave the homes and shtibelach in which they have been reared? Where shall they turn in their shtibel-less suburbia for anchorage, affiliation, and identification? We have already, unfortunately, seen the glimmer of an answer in present-day communities. It would seem that when the child is not trained to have a healthy regard for an orthodox shul; when there is discrimination engendered vis-à-vis the traditional synagogue, he cannot be discriminating when the time comes for *his* synagogue choice! This has been proven to the delight of the Conservative suburban temples and to our chagrin and shame.

One final, most important point. The Jew who is a congregant of a synagogue is constantly exposed to ideas, causes, and projects. He may react positively or negatively but he is aware of the community's problems, needs, hopes, and aspirations. Not only the community's, but that of the Jewish world — at home and abroad. His very presence in shul compels his involvement and this exposure makes him a responsible, sensitive, responding Jew. How tragic to witness some of the finest material we possess deliberately withdrawing themselves into a sound-proof, insulated, and isolated group. They are not exposed to the rabbi, to the appeals committee, the youth, and *limud Torah* committees. The voice of Israel does not penetrate their self-imposed barriers — and the community's needs and problems are conveniently sealed out. What horrible waste — the finest minds, the most sensitive ears, and the wisest hearts shut, closed, and dulled. The price for convenient, comfortable, self-righteous, gracious living is a most exorbitant one! On the other hand the price for acceptance of responsibility and community participation would be small in comparison — namely the sacrifice of vanity and pride.

Let it be made clear that the natural desire for a continued *chavruthah*, for companionship of *yeshivah-leit*, is commendable and need not be abandoned. It is beneficial and laudable. It should, however, not be to the exclusion of the synagogue. It should supplement — not supplant. Better yet — the *chavruthah* could well be the means of bringing the beth-hamidrosh back into the shul — to the benefit of all.

To anticipate the inevitable question, "Is the shul really the *most* important institution in a community?" we hasten to state that there are doubtless other areas more important — education and *taharath hamishpochah*, to mention but two. However, our thesis is that the building and maintaining of a day school can best be accomplished through an aware, dedicated group of men and women who are guided and directed from and through the shul. A mikvah project emanates from synagogue leaders and the rabbi. The atmosphere so necessary for the success of these projects is created by and through the synagogue. The vehicle best suited for all important endeavors — religious, educational, or philanthropic — is still the shul. Support of yeshivoth, of Israel, of all Torah projects, is rallied through the shul. Yes, there are more important institutions, but it is difficult to conceive of their establishment and maintenance without the synagogue as the central recruitment center of momentum, money, and manpower.

A wise man once said, "Friends are not made, they are recognized." An even wiser man, Solomon, said: *As in water face answereth face; so the heart of man to man* (Proverbs 27:19). One's reflection in water is blurred and unclear, unless you bend down and take a look. So it is if you wish to see your reflection in the pattern of the community. One must bend down a bit and take a long, careful look. If he does so, he will recognize his many friends there — and above all he will recognize and find himself. One is tempted to say to our yeshiva products, "Bend down a bit, and come on in — the water's fine!"

Chapter 7

# A Manual for Baale-Battim

Every fledgling rabbi, regardless of all the *seforim* he has accumulated since bar mitzvah, purchases a handbook such as "Hamadrich" upon entering the active rabbinate. Be it a wedding, funeral, unveiling, *b'rith milah*, or *pidyon haben*, it is imperative to have a handy guidebook which gives the *seder*, the proper order for that particular service. Torah scholarship, Halachic knowledge, even proficiency in Talmudic *pilpul* are no substitutes for the organized, catalogued, properly-presented protocol one finds in a rabbinic manual or handbook. It insures against the inadvertent faux-pas, it guides the novice safely through a path filled with pitfalls, and guarantees that required rules and regulations will be correctly observed.

The rabbi is well fortified and guarded against error and deviation thanks to his manual. But what of the innocent layman? Who shall protect the naive *baal habayis*, who means well but is untutored and unversed in his responsibilities and ignorant of what is expected of him during the most important moments of his life. The time has come, it seems to us, to present a "Handbook for Baale-Battim," a manual for the layman setting forth the procedure he should follow, when planning a wedding, a b'rith, a pidyon ha-ben, a bar mitzvah, or *cholilah* when a funeral must be arranged. The average layman often does not know how he should relate to his rabbi during these climactic moments of life, especially in larger Jewish communities where one may have a number of rabbis to invite, and where caterers determine availability of date and funeral directors the time best suited to their schedule. He does not know what is expected of him or how he should conduct himself.

The purpose of this chapter is to advise and guide him so he may

## A Manual for Baale-Battim

avoid the more common pitfalls, and to help him conduct himself with propriety, *derech eretz* — respectful conduct — and *seder*, correct procedure. Understandably, we will not be able to cover every eventuality or anticipate every problem, but we will attempt to address ourselves to some of the important moments of Jewish life and suggest the proper path to be pursued. Unquestionably many rabbis and laymen who will read this chapter will have their own suggestions and advice drawing upon their own unique experiences, which we will accept most graciously and in the same spirit of good-will that we write these lines. Our prime concern and purpose is to help prevent frictions in a community and avoid embarrassments which so often occur due only to lack of knowledge, oversight, and naivete.

A *simchah* in the family is a hectic and exciting occasion. Some allow for long-range planning such as a wedding and a bar mitzvah, whereas others, such as a b'rith milah, do not. A wedding usually permits a period of careful preparation and most people spend many months in attending to every detail so as to insure a beautiful affair. The hall is hired, as are the musicians and photographers. The invitations are ordered and dutifully mailed out six weeks in advance of the wedding date. Now the rabbi may or — strange as it may seem to some — may not have been notified of the date before he receives his printed invitation. Simple courtesy dictates that he should not be notified of an impending wedding of a congregant through the invitation alone. Derech-eretz for a rav demands that he be called or visited by the parents and formally invited to the wedding. This has ever been the traditional Jewish custom and it is most proper that this beautiful custom be continued.

It is also most important for the rabbi to meet with the couple well in advance of the wedding date to discuss with them a number of vital items. During this interview, he will not only have an opportunity to become better acquainted with them, but this intimate get-together will allow him to explain the significance of various aspects of the Jewish wedding ceremony and above all, he will use this occasion to discuss the *halochoth* of taharath hamishpochah, kashruth, and other laws which govern the Jewish home and family life.

Even though the rabbi may have been properly invited to the

wedding, how often, if ever, is he consulted *before* the date and time is selected? The caterer does not hesitate to inform his clients that their first choice, or even second, is taken and the parents hasten to choose the first open date available to them. They do not question the right of the caterer to be booked and hence unavailable. The rabbi, however, is presented with a fait accompli, this is the date and time of our daughter's wedding! But what if he is not available on that date or at that particular time? The mood of meek acceptance demonstrated by the parents in the caterer's office now strangely becomes transformed into an angry and hurt reaction at the rabbi's unwillingness or inability to fit into a schedule which conflicts with his prior commitments.

This insensitivity to the rabbi's position and role, which should merit priority, is often compounded by those who do not find it necessary to invite the rabbi to perform the ceremony or officiate in some way at the *chupah*. In New York, and doubtless in other large Jewish communities, far too often an angonizing game of chance is indulged in by congregational rabbis as they appear at the wedding wondering what part they are going to play. Basic respect for the rav requires that the *mechutan*, the father of the bride or groom, speak to him well in advance of the wedding and discuss with him his specific role at the simchah. It is advisable that he be informed as to who will be participating with him so that he can guide his congregant in arranging an orderly and dignified ceremony. Traditionally the rav of the groom is the *mesader kiddushin*. Other honors fitting for the rabbi of the bride and other dignitaries are the reading of the *kethubah*, the brief sermon under the chupah, and the various *sheva b'rochoth* as well as the *birchath hamozon* at the meal.

In recent years we have been blessed with roshey yeshivah, *rebbeyim* of the groom, and relatives who have *Semichah*, rabbinic ordination. It has become customary to honor the rosh yeshivah with the *Siddur Kiddushin* and to involve the *musmochim* who are relatives most prominently in the ceremony. At the risk of sounding heretical and shocking the sensibilities of b'ney yeshivah, these practices are questionable at best and at times prove to be most insulting to the kovod ho-rabonuth — the dignity and honor of the rabbinate. Historically and traditionally, siddur kiddushin is in the domain of the rav, not the rosh yeshivah and certainly not the principal, teacher, or businessman who happens to have graduated

## A Manual for Baale-Battim

from a yeshiva. Laymen must understand that the rabbi of a congregation and community is apt to be far more experienced in the application of the halochoth of kiddushin to conduct a wedding in a proper and orderly manner. He may, of course, grant the honor of being mesader kiddushin to a rosh yeshivah or a colleague who is related to the groom or bride but it is *his* right and privilege, not that of the *mechutonim*. A relation especially should understand, as should his family, that he comes to the wedding precisely in that capacity and it is discourteous and disrespectful to relegate one's own rabbi to a secondary role in the wedding of his congregant. A rosh yeshivah (incidentally a title which should not be used as lightly and loosely as it is today) is worthy of reverence and respect but not at the expense of the rav.

"A son of thirteen years to mitzvoth" is reason enough for celebration, but what kind of celebration? The place, the setting, the character of the simchah is all important. The boy is becoming a son of mitzvoth, not marking his puberty rites. The central focal point of this event, the single major observance of a bar mitzvah celebration, is, of course, the Shabboth morning service. It is then that the young man will be called to the Torah, manifesting his newly acquired role as a "godol," an adult responsible Jew. He may be fortunate enough to have mastered the reading of the Torah, so he will read the *Sedrah* in addition to being honored with the *Haftorah* or an *aliyah*. He may deliver a *D'var Torah* or a *pilpul* depending upon his knowledge and ability. It may not even be a Shabboth but a *Rosh Chodesh* or any day when the Torah is read, but *this* is the bar mitzvah — not the kiddush, the luncheon, the breakfast, or the banquet.

A conspiracy of silence has enveloped the bar mitzvah ritual in the United States and even in orthodox circles many are guilty of treating the "religious part" as secondary to the primary one, namely the "Affair." The Talmud teaches us that "the Torah is concerned for the money of Israel," not only for our souls but even for our pocketbooks! Generosity and open-handedness is to be commended when our means and possessions are used for proper purposes but it is questionable whether a lavish kiddush and an even more extravagant affair on a Saturday night or Sunday enhances the true spirit of reaching one's Jewish majority and accepting the yoke of mitzvoth. Though caterers may cry out in protest and some children complain, it will be well for some brave souls to curtail the exhorbitant expenses of a bar mitzvah celebration and use the money for a better cause.

This unseemly practice of conducting elaborate affairs to mark a bar mitzvah is compounded by the nature and character of some parties even among day school students. The non-Jewish spirit that pervades some of these affairs, the improper behavior and tawdry aspects, makes of the bar mitzvah event a travesty and mockery. To celebrate the reaching of the age of mitzvoth by spending an evening in indulging in *aveyroth* is shocking and shameful. Blessed will be those who are courageous enough to call a halt to these practices.

It is important to touch upon one other modern problem regarding bar mitzvah celebrations. True, many of the complexities of a wedding and the resultant problems we discussed are not applicable to a bar mitzvah, but there is one special point unique to this celebration that parents should ponder. Strangely, among observant Jews and B'nei Torah, more so than among non-orthodox Jews, it has become fashionable to celebrate the bar mitzvah Shabboth away from home in a hotel or resort rather than in the shul where the family attends services every Shabboth. There may be valid and legitimate reasons for this strange custom, such as the problem of accommodations for visitors and prevention of *chillul Shabboth*, but even so in many communities it has become so widespread that one is almost ashamed to have to celebrate his son's bar mitzvah in the shul.

Common sense, the honor of the beth ha-k'nesseth, and a sense of history should be of sufficient reason to convince Torah Jews of the importance of marking this event in a synagogue and not in the makeshift shul of a hotel. The rabbi of the congregation is also placed in a most embarrassing, delicate, and difficult position. He would like to share in the simchah of a congregant and friend but is it proper for him to leave the congregation in favor of a single congregant? Firstly, by so doing there is a depreciation of *kovod ha-tzibbur*, the honor due a congregation. Secondly, and perhaps far more important, he is encouraging, or at best accepting, a practice which is detrimental to the stature and status of the synagogue. The convenience and comfort of a hotel bar mitzvah is not of sufficient import to outweigh the sanctity that only a shul can offer, nor is it weighty enough to counteract the adverse lesson being given in derech eretz to the young lad. The place for this event is the shul where the young man has been reared and where his parents daven every Shabboth.

The celebration of a b'rith milah and a pidyon ha-ben do not present the complexity of problems which confront the planning of a wedding and a bar mitzvah. A comparatively shorter period of time for planning is entailed. Nonetheless, the laws and customs are in some ways more intricate and the layman should be made aware of some of these laws as well as the niceties and subtleties involved in the ceremony and the honors. The *Mohel* obviously plays a most important role and where there is an option and choice in his selection the rabbi should be asked for his opinion rather than depending upon a friend's recommendation. There are modern methods used by mohelim today, many of them questionable halachically, and the rav is the one to check with *before* the mohel is retained.

The honors available at a b'rith are varied and permit for distribution among relatives and friends at the circumcision. The most important honor is that of *sandek*, the one who holds the infant on his lap during the circumcision. This honor is traditionally given to the rav, the grandfather, or the great-grandfather, the latter being preferable to the former but neither taking precedence over the rav. Here again in recent years, due to lack of knowledge or negligence, the rabbi is often bypassed and not necessarily for the substitution of a grandfather but for any relative or friend. Only one generation ago this was unheard of, that the *Morah D'assrah* should not be invited to serve as the sandek. Unfortunately, this is one more example of the lessening of kovod ho-rabonuth, due in many cases to the lack of knowledge of baale-battim.

A pidyon ha-ben does not normally present the special problems common to a wedding, bar mitzvah, or b'rith, but laymen should be cautioned that not every Kohen is conversant with the halochoth or procedure of the Redemption of the First-born Son. The rav should be consulted regarding any questions including the selection of a Kohen and the exact order to be followed in the pidyon.

## A Manual for Baale-Battim

We have touched upon *simchoth*, the joyous moments of life, now let us turn our attention to the final climactic moment — death. The shock and grief attendant upon death makes the planning of the funeral most difficult. It also means that the family is vulnerable and in a state of disarray. It is therefore extremely important that in arranging a funeral proper procedures be followed and extreme care exercised. The widespread abuses and violations of Torah law and Jewish tradition by funeral directors, abetted by public ignorance and apathy, is well known by all sensitive and intelligent Jews. In addition to these religious transgressions, the American way of death with much of its vulgarity and lack of propriety and dignity has also permeated the Jewish community and must be combatted. The Union of Orthodox Jewish Congregations and other groups, rabbinic and lay, have in recent years faced up to many of these improper practices and brought a degree of order into an area where anarchy reigned unchallenged for far too long. Nonetheless, no force is as powerful as that of the public, or to be more specific in this case, the client. It is imperative that Jewish families resist the pressures of friends, the persistence of casket salesmen, and the subtle seductions of society which militate against the simple dignity of Jewish law and practice.

The congregation that has an active *Chevrah Kadishah* is fulfilling one of the major functions of an orthodox synagogue. They will prove to be a bulwark of aid and comfort in this most trying time in a family's experience. They will not only attend to the necessary preparations but also act as a buffer between the family and the professional funeral directors. The rav is always a tower of strength at this moment, not only in bringing solace and condolence to the bereaved family but in overseeing the *taharah, tachrichim*, and the kashruth of the coffin. Not only are these basics to be treated with care and caution but the funeral arrangements as well.

The time set for the funeral is unfortunately often done arbitrarily and the rabbi is expected to be available without any consideration for his schedule, a conflict which could be avoided by consulting him *before* the time is set. Another delicate area, in larger communities, is the failure on the part of the family to invite the rabbi to officiate at or participate in the funeral service. Often there are others involved in the service and the rabbi of the bereaved family's congregation is at a loss as to his role. Courtesy and derech eretz require the family to ask their rabbi to either conduct the service or to deliver one of the eulogies. A rabbi may at times attend a funeral as a friend of the family without participating, but in his *official* capacity he will not appear at the Chapel unless invited by the family. Nor is it the function of the rabbi to attend all services at the house of the mourner if he attends regular services, morning and evening, at the synagogue. The tzibbur is more important than the individual and doubtless there are laymen who can help organize and conduct the daily minyon at the mourner's house. In general it is the rabbi's role to give direction and decisions in all matters pertaining to the preparations for a funeral and the Shivah period. It is the role of baale-battim to occupy themselves with duties such as *shemirah* (watching), taharah, the meal of condolence, and arranging the services in the house of mourning.

The division of labor and responsibility between rabbi and layman is not a clearly defined one. It certainly is not a rigid, inflexible one. However, there are, or should be, those which fall into the domain of the rav's authority and responsibility while others are the responsibility of the layman. Above all let there not be the invasion of the former by the latter or the abdication on the part of baale-battim, in favor of the rabbi, when their fullest participation is essential.

There are two areas which merit mention, for they have proven to be among the most troublesome in recent years — kashruth and taharath ha-mishpochah. The rabbi obviously is charged to oversee these vital areas. He must provide leadership, guidance, and constant supervision. Nonetheless, the laity is not relieved from responsibility in these areas for they are not the exclusive domain of the rabbinate. They belong to k'lal Yisroel. In far too many communities the budget, the mechanics of operation, and the daily administration of these important services fall completely upon the shoulders of the rabbi. This is unfair and unjust and may eventually lead to the weakening and even disruption of these services. The baale-battim who care, must deem it a distinct honor and privilege to assume the burden of administering the communal program for these two fundamental mitzvoth that are so vital to the viability of a Jewish community.

There are many other examples of the relationship between

layman and rabbi, as well as between the layman and the community, which we have not focused upon. Organizational protocol also at times require tact and taste. Should the rabbi or his wife be approached to participate financially in certain congregational functions or serve actively on a committee? We have not chosen to discuss these and similar questions for we feel that there are no common guidelines. Discretion and good judgment will doubtless dictate the correct and proper behavior. We have attempted in this chapter to suggest what we consider to be a correct mode of behavior on the part of baale-battim in certain areas which are common to many, if not all, kehiloth and which represent those moments of life where the layman and rabbi are most apt to come into close, direct contact with each other.

The suggestions made are not halochoth — they are not part of the four sections of the Shulchon Oruch. They *do* belong to the "fifth" one, which traditionally is the name given for the section (unwritten) that deals with common sense and common courtesy. In all human relationship life is made bearable and tolerable by mutual consideration and understanding. This is true of families, the business and professional worlds, and wherever the social contract is kept as part of the unwritten law which governs and controls the society of man. It most certainly should be cheerfully accepted and scrupulously observed in guiding the relationship of baale-battim to their community, congregation, and rabbi.

The ways of Torah are ways of pleasantness. Derech eretz preceded Torah, hence it is the introduction and the entrance to the ways of peace and pleasantness. The People of the Book must study the introduction to the Book and model their lives accordingly. There is a saying that when a true thought enters your mind it gives a light which allows you to see many other concepts which one never perceived before. Hopefully the consideration and practice of the simple but important rules of courtesy and derech eretz presented here will help our fellow Jews realize the importance of acting with propriety and respect in their responsible respected roles as baale-battim.

Part II

# Issues of Our Time

# Introduction

The purpose of Torah is to teach man a "derech ha'chayim" — a way of life. How to behave in his private life, how to conduct himself in relationship to his fellowman and how to serve G-d in his every action and deed. The disciplines of Torah are all encompassing, touching upon every aspect of man's existence. The Torah, however, does not tell us to 'be good' but commands us to 'be holy!' Holiness is not a rejection of this world but its affirmation, not isolation from society but involvement, not a begrudging co-existence with man's needs and nature's laws but a joyful acceptance of all G-d has granted us, with the realization that we are to sanctify, hallow and ennoble it.

Secular society, humanist philosophy and the pleasure principle of modern man has distorted so much of our thinking that it is imperative we learn how to view human behavior, morality, the world of nature, and the role of woman from a Torah perspective. Too many of us have allowed the media to mold our attitudes, secular scholars to shape our social standards, and the pressures of society to impose upon us a life style which is alien to the disciplines of Torah and Halacha.

In the following chapters we will address ourselves to a number of issues confronting us in today's world which in our opinion have been obfuscated and often distorted by modern mores and secular pundits. We will present the Torah perspective on such vital matters as morality and the pressures exerted on home and family by a society devoid of kedusha. It is also imperative to consider how Torah views the sex roles and the relationship of man to nature. Finally we will comment on what is probably the greatest threat to the sanctity and purity of the k'lal Yisroel — the scourge of

*Introduction*

intermarriage. Hopefully by shedding light on these topics we can help guide the reader to reach the goal envisioned for k'lal Yisroel — to be a kingdom of priests and a holy people.

## Chapter 8

# Rebels — Because . . .

Historians often give a name to a period of history which captures in succinct fashion the true temper of that time, reflecting the authentic image of an era. Contemporaries are too close to rapidly changing events to properly evaluate the true character of the current scene. Not so today, however, for we know that future historians will call our present period—"The Age of the Youth Rebellion."

The rebellion of youth has been developing at a fast pace since the end of World War II. We see it above all on the campus, although the spirit manifests itself on many varied fronts, including the family circle. It intrudes into many areas: fashion, the lively arts, literature and language, mores and morals.

The slogans on the banners under which rebellious youth marches vary. Anti-war, anti-establishment, and anti-age (which includes all those over thirty). Pro-freedom, liberty, and equality as defined by their hero of the moment, be he Mao, Che Guevara, or Malcolm X. Above all the cry is for change—tear down the old, the sick, the decadent, and build anew. To some even this is not sufficient and the red flag of revolution is torn down, replaced by the black flag of anarchy. The frightening thing is that there are some who respond by hoisting the white flag of surrender. The majority, however, react with the plaintive cry, "What do they want?" The more thoughtful attempt to analyze the causes of this restlessness and disruption offering remedies and panaceas.

This much is certain: all are concerned, for none can reasonably be detached and apathetic. To ignore the rebellious spirit would be folly, to dismiss it as a passing trend would be tragic, to panic would

## Rebels — Because...

be disastrous. Certainly we Jews, as part of society at large, must attempt to answer the question "What do they want?" and seek the basic causes while exploring the possible way out, but we must do so from our unique, particular, Torah point of view. Freedom and liberty are concepts which flow from our tradition and teachings. Alienation is a feeling we know too well. Fear and frustration have been our companions for centuries and the pages of our history are filled with dissent. Change is part of our fabric and the revolutionary spirit was kindled in Canaan before it glowed in the United States and France—certainly in Russia and Asia. We do have something of importance and value to say from the perspective of Torah, in a broader sense than the prophetic teachings of social justice and the rights of all mankind.

We will address ourselves to three basic issues involved in recent events and to some of the areas of conflict which concern us all, with special emphasis upon the campus community. We will attempt to examine some of those concepts and ideas which confront society in a most profound way for they are ideas which go to the very heart of the issues with which we must come to grips. They are the questions of (1) Freedom and liberty versus discipline and authority; (2) The role of education; and (3) Youth versus Age.

Youthful rebellion is no new phenomenon. The generation gap is quite natural. Our Rabbis recognize this division and separation of interest, depicting it in the famous story of Choni, the Jewish Rip van Winkle, who, upon his return after a lengthy slumber found his generation gone and cried out: "Give me comradeship or grant me death." Realistically, the older and younger generation cannot be equals and they certainly cannot be pals. They can, however, be cooperative, thereby insuring continuity. The key to their relationship is the recognized authority of parents, teachers, and elders with "derech eretz" the guarantor of meaningful respect and a sense of responsibility the fruits of this relationship. This does not mean that for centuries we lived in an authoritarian society. It does mean that the classic Jewish home is one where parents listen to their children but don't submit while children speak to their parents but don't talk back. The lines of communication are open because there is a common language, a common sense of values, and a common code by which they all live.

## Rebels — Because . . .

The moral and social order of the Jewish home and family, as well as that of society and community, was ever regulated by Torah law, guided by teachings which were accepted because they were revered, insuring the stability of family and community. As long as parents adhere to a code of law, honest in their convictions and fair in their dealings with their children, discipline is present in the household, not through coercion but in an atmosphere of liberty. What a noted Italian educator has pointed out is very true of our concept of freedom and discipline—two elements which are not in conflict but complement one another: "Discipline to be meaningful must come *through* liberty. It does not mean that one becomes silent and docile, accepting without question, obeying without doubt. When discipline is founded upon liberty, it itself is active, not passive."

The Jewish home and the ideal Torah society is certainly not passive and quiet. It is alive, vibrant, and at times unruly. There is, however, an underlying acceptance of authority, a readiness to act responsibly without the need for repressive action. Above all there is a sense of respect and reverence which gives a special flavor and grace to the discipline under which men live. This ingredient is all important to an understanding of our *hashkofah*, our attitude and point of view. The three R's of education—reading, 'riting, and 'rithmetic—have given way, unfortunately, in some educational institutions to riots, rampage, and revolt. The reason for this may well be the eclipsing of what education is supposed to implant and teach as the corollary three R's; respect, responsibility, and reverence.

It is admittedly difficult to revere the elementary three R's. It is most natural for a Jew committed to the Covenant to revere Torah. It is also quite natural to cry out for change; it is difficult to deny it unless there are rules and regulations, values and standards, ideas and ideals that are unchanging. The demand for change is legitimate if change is necessary and will improve the condition and conduct of man and society. The danger lies in a demand for indiscriminate change including the casting off of valued and tested truths that are the foundation of order and stability in the moral and social realm. Change is not the panacea to problems any more than dissent in itself is sacred. The *right* to dissent is sacred and the machinery for change is vital but mature judgment and wise evaluation are pre-requisites for both dissent and change. There is a tendency at times to equate change and progress, whereas the two are not synonymous. There is also the erroneous inclination to look upon all innovations as acts of creativity. True creativity has been defined as taking a fresh clean look at old truths. This is an exercise which we have abandoned in recent years and one which we would do well to revive. Creativity is never dulled by age, only by disuse.

Understandably it is youth that champions change. This is logical and reasonable, resulting from their enthusiastic temperament. True, youth is enthusiastic and age is at times lethargic. Youth is dissatisfied and age overly complacent. "The errors of enthusiasm may even be preferable to the indifference of wisdom," as Anatole France said, but there is also the prudence of wisdom and the insanity of anarchy to be considered. The latter is certainly the fruit of unbridled enthusiasm. Events at Columbia University and other colleges in recent years, point up the perils of permissiveness which are nigh impossible to control as they erupt into violence. Muscle soon dominates over mind and the spectacle of collegiate storm troopers is a chilling one. Power is the prize sought and if power corrupts it would seem that the smell of power perverts. Protest too easily can spill over into insurrection and anarchy. It is an ugly sight to observe students intimidating and blackmailing university administrations, and cowing fellow students.

It is difficult to determine the exact motivation of many students who participate in demonstrations. Perhaps it is one part exasperation, one part exuberance, and one part exhibitionism. This breakdown of respect for authority and dissipation of discipline on campus, however, is not an isolated image of rebellious youth. It has well been said that youth does not create an image, rather it reflects it. Doubtless this disruption of institutions of higher learning reflects the temper of the times. But we must recognize it as symptomatic of weaknesses and shortcomings of modern education in general.

The shortcomings in the field of higher education today are threefold: the lost art of teaching, the lack of an established ethic, and the abdication of authority. To paraphrase a quip attributed to Gandhi, who when asked what he thought of western civilization answered, "I think it is a good idea," we would answer likewise if asked what we thought of higher education today. There is a disquieting reluctance to engage in the actual act of teaching in our universities. It seems to be the ambition of almost every instructor and assistant professor to reduce his teaching load and engage in research and writing. When he does teach he does not necessarily instruct, inspire, or influence—for that would be contrary to the cherished principle of allowing every student to make up his own mind and reach his own decision and conclusion. He rather explores together with his class the subject at hand, carefully avoiding the pitfall of imposing ideas. He assiduously presents all points of view and alternatives lest he be guilty of indoctrination and dogmatism. This does not mean that there are no professors who impose their ideology upon their students. There are, and they are in most cases adherents of the radical-liberal-activist school. As such they are in no small measure responsible for the riots of the 60s by contributing to, and even fostering, the antagonistic attitudes of those who occupy university buildings, destroy private papers, and defy law and authority. The ridiculous extremes to which non-instruction has been carried, for fear of being dogmatic, is apparently waived if power is controlled by students and intimidation exercised by youth.

The reluctance to instruct lest it be indoctrination, to guide and direct lest it be dubbed doctrinaire, may also be due to the fact that there is no real ethic, no set of moral principles, no system of values or rules of conduct to which the academician adheres. Hence, what discipline, what code shall he teach as the embodiment of truth? Again, this is so with the exception of negative dogmatism and one's own prejudiced principles. For example, a few years ago, the Jewish counsellor at Columbia (an appointee of the university, not representing the Jewish community) challenged the right to pass judgment on the scandalously immoral behaviour of students at the university, even to the extent of intervening on behalf of a student guilty of flagrant defiance of university rules, yet vigorously castigated the administration for refusing amnesty to those students who rioted and destroyed university property. For such as he, the refusal was to be condemned while the immorality practiced in the disruption and near destruction of a university and the moral cowardice of refusal to accept one's punishment as consequence of one's deliberate acts were to be condoned. That these actions were supposedly motivated by high ideals serves but to heighten the immorality in asking for amnesty since what was done was purportedly motivated by the passion of conscience. A sad commentary indeed on the moral fiber of modern martyrs!

Guilty as educators may be in their non-instruction and in their lack of ethic to guide them, college administrators are no less guilty in their abdication of authority. The Leclaire Case, alluded to before in conjunction with Columbia's Jewish chaplain, is a case in point. The president of Barnard College assures us all that no action will be taken against this girl for breaking house rules by cohabiting with a young man off campus. That college presidents are reluctant to become guardians of moral codes, sanctioned by all religious faiths and concurred in by civilized society for many centuries, is perhaps understandable. What *is* incomprehensible is the fear manifested by college authorities in enforcing their *own* rules! The refusal of college administrators to exercise their authority and enforce university rules and regulations cannot fail but to impress upon students that one can violate them with impunity, thereby encouraging the extension of violation to violence and of defiance to disruption and destruction.

The dissipation of respect, the contempt for the establishment, uncivil disobedience, disdain and ridicule of moral codes and standards of behavior are the result of a failure to properly educate our young people and to give them direction to cultivate a sense of adherence to authority. Youth, however, desperately needs both direction and authority. Above all they need some code which they can respect and cling to. To fill the vacuum created by the failure of universities to fill this need, energies and loyalties are perforce rechanneled. Alien ideologies, often dangerous and self-defeating, are sought out and enthusiastically embraced.

The pictures adorning the ivy-covered buildings of Columbia University during the seizures of the 60s were those of Mao, Che Guevara, and Malcolm X. These were their heroes. Not Socrates or Plato, not even Darwin and Freud, but the apostles of revolution and violence. To us this is even more tragic if we accept the figure given by Time magazine that fifty percent of those involved in campus activism are Jews. To be so estranged from the fundamentals, not only of Judaism but of responsible humanism and the classical liberal spirit, is appalling. To cast one's lot with forces which have

## Rebels — Because . . .

displayed their contempt of, and enmity to, the Jewish people is grotesque. There is a special Jewish stake involved in the rebellious spirit of our time, for this spirit rejects many of the basic fundamental laws of decency, fair play, and tolerance which create a climate necessary to the growth and progress of Jewish communities. Antisemitism grows and flourishes in the soil of extremism and is nurtured in an atmosphere of recklessness and anarchy. Stability and order, respect for authority and law, have ever been the ingredients necessary for our security and our rights as Jews in the Diaspora. Racism, white or black, turmoil on the campuses, and the "New Left" have a common denominator for us—they are not "Good For The Jews" nor do they contribute to the wellbeing of society at large. Mature responsible Jewish leadership appreciates this full well. Adult Jews, to whatever degree perceptive and sharp politically, sense it, while much of youth, unfortunately, has yet to learn this lesson which our history has taught us time and time again.

But beyond the direct consequences to our Jewish community, we must also consider the special stake we have in the moral fibre and health of the society in which we live. We are influenced by our environment, our children are deeply affected by the general atmosphere around them, and we in turn have a special responsibility to help fashion the community in which we live. We have never been absolved from our mission to be a "holy nation and a kingdom of priests," even in exile.

When we observe the real sickness of modern society, not only its violence and vulgarity which are but symptoms of the illness but the erosion of ethics and the methodical destruction of moral codes by which civilized man has always lived, then we realize this unique obligation we have as Torah Jews to combat this sickness. We certainly should not be partners to those who foster this illness and above all we must do all we can to dissuade our own young people from lending their talents and energies to these elements. On the contrary, we must do all in our power to strengthen those forces which represent responsibile adherence to law, order, and decency in our communities. These are the forces that enabled the establishment of communities in which Jewish institutions have flourished, whereas that which is represented by the other forces will destroy all

## Rebels — Because . . .

that we have built over the years.

The spirit of rebellion, the dissent and questioning displayed by youth, need not be stifled—on the contrary, it should be encouraged, for it contains the seeds of hope and change for the future. It has but to be properly channeled and utilized. We as Torah Jews have no reason to fear this spirit for it may well be the beginning of a renewed progress toward the sources of our traditions. If materialism is being challenged, if the values of our generation are being questioned, then the ideals and principles of our generation are also being rejected and therein lies the hope for our community and for society in general. Certainly the past generation did not give much allegiance to the principles and teachings of Torah. It was precisely their preoccupation with the Golden Calf that caused such massive alienation from Torah discipline on the part of today's parents. Ironically, it is this same debased sense of values which is causing the alienation of *their* children from the "establishment."

Young people desperately need someone and something they can believe in and trust. They seek out that which they can admire and even revere. Unfortunately they do not always find the way which will lead them to their proper heroes and ideals. Yet, there are an appreciable number who have rebelled against the mores and standards of their parents and found themselves not in Greenwich Village but in the halls of yeshivoth and eventually in the mainstream of the Torah community. Admittedly they represent a minor percentage of the totality but what interests us is that they exist at all! The spirit of rebellion must not be destroyed but captured, not tamed but properly utilized.

In the concluding Mishnah of Mesechta Soteh we read: "In the footsteps of the Messiah, insolence will increase and honor dwindle. Youths will put old men to shame, the old will stand up in the presence of the young; a son will revile his father, a daughter will rise up against her mother, and a man's enemies will be the members of his household." Many will agree that we are within hearing distance of the footsteps of the Messiah, if this be the indication of his coming. We must not, however, be misled into thinking that we will abet the coming of the Messiah by encouraging the fulfillment of this Mishnah. Our responsibility is still that of rearing children who have respect for their elders and realize that the period of youth

## Rebels — Because . . .

is one of preparation for adulthood when fulfillment will be theirs. Unfortunately we are the heirs of a lengthy period of permissiveness in the raising of children. A wit put it well when he said that the accent may be on youth but the stress is on the adult. Judaism does not, however, look upon age as automatically possessing all the answers, just as it does not have great regard for the wisdom of youth. We have ever attempted to strike a proper balance wherein we appreciate the maturing of wisdom with the passage of time while admiring the exuberance and enthusiasm of youth. The Talmud (Mesechtah Shabboth) states, perhaps with tongue in cheek: "There is no reason in old men and no counsel in children." Experience is no substitute for wisdom, which explains the first part of their aphorism but by the same token youth does not have all the answers, which is the interpretation of the latter part of our Sages' remark.

Knowing, then, that the answer to the problems which vex us today can be found in the teachings of our Torah and Sages, we can realize that the application of the answer is in the climate of a society fashioned by men, women, and children who conduct themselves in accordance with the code of Torah. As a people we developed a fine sense of freedom and liberty which was always intense but which somehow never interfered with our acceptance of the most exacting regulations and disciplines. This blending of liberty and discipline carried over from the religious realm to the temporal. The Jew, trained to obey and accept authority in his own private life established a habit pattern which then was applied to his relationship, in various countries, to a variety of governments and regimes. This does not mean that he ever accepted tyranny. History shows that Jews never ceased to believe in, and fight for, equality and liberty. The ability to strike this delicate balance between liberty and license was seriously impeded as Jews cast off the religious disciplines in the private realm. Only by a process of education and training in the discipline of mitzvoth can we teach our young people to intelligently evaluate their responsibility to government on the one hand and the needs of a free society on the other

The best resistance to irresponsible and dangerous ideologies is still intelligence. Our young people are certainly blessed with this gift. Some, however, have unhappily squandered it as they have been denied the rich treasure of heritage which is theirs. Although they would proclaim their independence, nonetheless they march so often to the beat of another man's drum. All of us must march to some beat. Fortunately we Jews have been given a rhythm and a destination. Unfortunately, many have developed a tin ear and a faulty sense of direction.

The major need of the moment is not only to educate, train, and teach but to inspire, guide, and direct our young people, to convince them that our times can be attuned to the spirit of Torah, that change must be measured by virtues and constants which are unchanging and that freedom and discipline are not in conflict. There is much talk today of *power* but not enough consideration given to *influence*. The former can be corrupt and corrupting, whether it be the establishment or the anti-establishment who exercise it. The latter is the key to all intelligent progress and decent human relationship. Power in itself de-humanizes, whereas an appreciation of the power of influence ennobles. To gain the power of influence one must however learn, grow, develop, and mature. For all this, one needs proper home environment, excellent schooling, and a healthy, forward-looking community. It is this alone that can build a better future for all of us.

One hears on many sides the call for "law and order." Candidates for high office base their campaign upon this platform. What we must realize, however, is that law represents a public expression of what society considers right and necessary but this does not guarantee compliance with and obedience to the law. Only if private persuasion is coupled with this public expression can law be meaningful. As for order, Burke put it very well at the close of the eighteenth century: "Society cannot exist unless a controlling power upon will and appetite be placed somewhere, and the less of it there is within, the more there must be without." We must bend every effort to establish law based upon private persuasion, and order by reconstituting man within, rather than without. This has ever been the Derech Ha-Torah.

Chapter 9

# The Lost Art of Derech Eretz

The recent troubles besetting the public schools of New York City, with comparable woes prevalent in other large urban areas, and the startling statistics of youthful crime, have once again focused our attention upon the ever recurring and painful problem of juvenile delinquency, acts of violence, and a general state of chaos in our modern society, among our adolescent population. A general deterioration of discipline against established authority has aroused our grave concern and resulted in articles, discourses, grand jury investigations, and charges breeding counter-charges, all attempting to discover the cause and root of this decline of basic elementary law and order in our communities.

It is not our purpose to propose a solution or find a panacea for the real and aggravated problem of terror in the public school system, or to judge the wisdom or lack of good sense in the mass suspension of incorrigibles from the classroom. Nor will we attempt to suggest how to deal with young criminals. We would rather discuss what is felt to be the very core of this entire question of adolescent rebellion as it affects all of us, whether we be among the unfortunates who are confronted directly with this problem or the more blessed ones who feel that their house is in order. We would direct our analysis to the general question of respect, or to use a phrase which speaks so much more eloquently—"Derech Eretz."

This hallowed virtue, now threatened with eclipse, is one which affects the lives of all, adults as well as adolescents and children. Its decline is keenly felt even in those circles which cannot be characterized by the stock phrases of "broken homes," "economically depressed neighborhoods," or even religiously neutral households.

## The Lost Art of Derech Eretz

The perceptive observer of the American scene must be cognizant of a general deterioration of respect and discipline in many areas—the home, the school, the house of worship, and the community. This alarming trend is to be observed not alone in the general American environment but also in the Jewish world. How shall we account for the rapidly changing atmosphere of the Jewish home, even including the orthodox household, wherein the attribute of derech eretz is becoming a lost art? What is the true picture of parent-child relationship and how are we to explain it? Our day schools have increased and enrollment is at a record high, but what are the true facts regarding derech eretz of yeshivah students for their teachers? Rabbis have attained a status of economic security and community prestige supposedly surpassing any period of Jewish history of the past century, but what is the real attitude of the laity—men, women and youngsters—towards their spiritual leaders? Is there indeed a sincere spirit of respect, reverence, obedience, and discipline? These are the demanding questions of our time which cannot be evaded but which require a full and frank appraisal.

The home in Jewish tradition has unquestionably been regarded as the stronghold of our people. The strange and alien winds of a hostile and often brutal world could never penetrate the house of Israel. Within the walls of the truly Jewish home reign serenity, peace, and warmth. It is not only a place of shelter from the elements, both natural and human, but a fortress of the spirit as well. It is the training ground of our youth, more so than the school, for within its confines Torah is taught not theoretically but *l'maaseh*. In word and in deed, the Jewish home has created an atmosphere molding and shaping the character attitudes, values, and standards of the young.

Among the virtues and attributes which have traditionally permeated the Jewish home, imbuing its members with its teachings, is of course the *midah* of derech eretz. This element of respect is all-embracing, affecting the behavior pattern of parents and children alike. The traditional home is parent- and elder-centered. Throughout the ages, Jewish children have been cherished, love has been lavished upon them, and a sense of security implanted within them from infancy, without benefit of books on child psychology. The child, however, has not been made the center of the truly Jewish home; never was he the hub of the wheel around which revolved the activity or motivation of the family. The head of the household was ever the father, to whom all looked for guidance, authority, and leadership. The attitude of the wife and husband toward each other is a major factor, for it serves as an object lesson for the children insofar as derech eretz is concerned. Mutual recognition and respect, deference and consideration as displayed by the parents, implant within the children a spirit of regard and reverence toward both, which serves as an excellent preparation for conveying this attitude toward their elders and superiors outside of the home. This disciplined spirit is logically transferred to teacher, rabbi, and communal authority, emanating as it does from the center of the home to the periphery of society and its established institutions. In other words, an adult-centered home developed an attitude which quite naturally affects every aspect of life experienced by the child.

This spirit of derech eretz has historically manifested itself not only in the parent-parent and parent-child relationship, but also in the attitude of the elders to certain standards and values of life and toward the exponents or symbols of these values. Children are impressionable and receptive. They sense their parents' approbation or disdain, their acceptance and admiration or disparagement and irreverence. The home wherein parents hold Torah standards, the teacher, rabbi, and authority in esteem and regard, is bound to inculcate these attitudes in their children. A home where Torah knowledge, piety, modesty, and sincerity are valued and revered, serves to imbue the children with the same spirit. The yardstick used by adults to measure the goal and objective of life, their definition of happiness, success, and fulfillment, will ever be applied by those who are exposed to this spirit, in their own endeavors.

Granted that this description of the traditional Jewish home, the spirit that has pervaded it and impressed itself upon the outside community, is authentic and correct, we can proceed to examine the condition of the Jewish home today and its effect upon other areas of human relationship. While many American Jewish homes have, *Boruch Hashem*, preserved this spirit, the average American Jewish home today, to the contrary, presents at times a curious and disturbing picture. Instead of being parent-centered many families have become child-centered. The expression "for the children" has become a familiar refrain. The child is the focal point of the household, with practically every activity revolving around him. Every effort is extended to make life comfortable and convenient for the offspring, and this is often accomplished at the expense of the dignity and position of the parents themselves. The emphasis in general today is upon youth, to such an extent that maturity, age, and even wisdom are relegated to an inferior position. Responsibility, obligation, and acceptance of a yoke are little known to the child or adolescent in the average so-called middle class Jewish household. How then can a spirit of derech eretz for the elder be engendered? The spirit of condescension or at best tolerance displayed by the adolescent toward the adult is no mere accident nor the strange fruit of a world we have not created. The roots are in the home and the fruits are those of the seeds planted from the initial phases of child development.

The decline of discipline and respect can also be traced, to a great extent, to the quasi-matriarchal society which we have seemingly fallen heir to in our modern American culture. Without reaching the radical conclusions of the exponents of the philosophy of "momism", one must reluctantly admit to the rapidly declining status of the husband and father in twentieth-century society. Too often our "women of valor" are guilty, albeit unconsciously and without malice aforethought, of casting the father into a position of inferiority and disesteem. The leveling of the sexes which has progressed so rapidly in recent years has taken its toll of the "head of the household" concept, which is so very important in implanting a spirit of derech eretz in the home in particular and society in general. Jewish tradition has always granted major status to the wife and mother, recognizing fully well her important, inimitable role in rearing her children and guiding them in their formative years. The central authority of the father, however, was inviolate and joyfully accepted. Authority and discipline cannot ultimately be shared; in the final analysis it must be embodied in one person.

By returning to the father his rights and responsibilities as the true head of the family we shall be taking a major step toward re-establishing the proper spirit of discipline and respect in the home. This in turn will certainly result in a greater efficacy of derech eretz

## The Lost Art of Derech Eretz

in other areas outside of the home.

Let us now consider the school and above all the teacher; the dedicated, consecrated, much maligned and little appreciated pedagogue. What degree of respect for him or her is fostered and nurtured in the average home? The educator is disrobed of his prestige and esteem when the true value of Torah and her standard bearers are spoken of disparagingly around the dinner table. How many Jewish parents are guilty of this far too common indoor sport? The rebbe cannot become an object of reverence if even a shadow of ridicule or deprecation is cast upon him in the home and his qualities of knowledge and piety will not be appreciated by the youngster if these values are not recognized and respected by his parents. This may seem an overly harsh and ill-considered indictment, yet let parents search their hearts frankly and honestly and determine whether they are indeed innocent of these actions. Only by creating an attitude of respect and regard toward the faculty of a school can there be proper discipline on the part of the children toward their teachers *in* the school.

There are two other disturbing developments which have manifested themselves on the American Jewish scene which warrant our considered attention. These are the spirit of democracy in religious life and the modern version of hero worship.

The Jew, since his acceptance of the yoke of mitzvoth at Sinai, has been a disciplined individual. This admirable virtue has been extolled in lore, legend and song. Moral suasion has ever been the great deterrent cultivated from childhood as the potent weapon against transgression and violation of law. In the realm of religious law the Jew has looked to Torah authority for guidance and direction. The eternal laws of Torah, with flexibility and adaptability inherent in the unique structure of halochah, have served as his code, with the only questions being the *Shaalah* which he presented to the rabbi for a *Teshuvah*. What was true of the individual was hitherto also accepted procedure for every congregation. The laws of synagogue practice, the standards of the house of prayer, have been those of the Shulchan Aruch; derech eretz for the decisions of the code as interpreted by the rav was ever the norm.

In recent years, however, we have witnessed the startling spectacle of subjecting questions of halochah—religious law and usage—to votes of lay memberships. The concept of majority rule, which never applied to questions of Jewish religious law insofar as the laity was concerned, has made a travesty of synagogue sanctity. Whether it be mixed seating, or various questionable social functions in the synagogue, all these have become issues to be decided on a par with budget or similar items on the agenda.

The rabbi has in many cases abdicated his authority and responsibility, with resultant chaos and confusion. This abdication cannot, however, be too severely condemned when we consider the great pressures brought to bear by individuals who control the personal security and future of the rabbi. This flouting of the authority of the rav has taken its toll among many members of the community, undermining reverence and respect toward the spiritual leader. The deterioration of derech eretz in the school and community can be attributed to a great extent to this distorted democratization of the synagogue. Not until the rightful role of teacher and interpreter of law is restored to the rabbi can we hope for a favorable improvement of respect and derech eretz in all areas of synagogue activity and in the relationship of layman and rabbi.

A discussion of the art of derech eretz would not be complete without one final observation, regarding hero-worship. Since the dawn of history man has felt a certain emotional hunger and need for an object of adulation. There has ever been a desire for emulation of and identification with a superior symbol. Hero-worship is the ultimate in the area of reverence and regard. We have no argument with any human emotion, especially one that is seemingly so deeply rooted in the consciousness of the individual. We do, however, feel that it is important to note whom our youngsters establish as their symbol of adulation and reverence today.

Our environment and culture is so constituted that our youngsters' feeling of respect and esteem, coupled with a desire for emulation and identification, is directed toward the glamorous stars of movies, TV, and the sports world. Parents and teachers must realize that although this hero-worship is quite natural, shallow and superficial as it may be, nonetheless this intense adulation cannot be squandered upon the rock-and-roll artist or home-run hitter without decreasing and diminishing the reservoir of awe and reverence within the youngster vis-à-vis others. We must give most serious consideration toward devising intelligent ways and means, in the school and the home, of re-channeling this inherent desire and need for hero-worship toward personalities and figures who are our true "gedolim". Our history abounds with spiritual giants and dramatic, colorful personalities who could well supplant the relatively drab, colorless, and insignificant objects of our children's adulation and esteem. A conscious, well-planned effort should be made to direct the attention of our children to these Jewish heroes, thereby imbuing them with a healthy spirit of respect for men and women of Jewish stature. This in turn would enhance their derech eretz for the values and philosophy of life which these personalities reflect.

The age we live in is one marked by tension, turbulence, and disruption. It is an age wherein man has split the atom, harnessed the forces of nature, conquered outer space, and discovered the means and powers which can destroy him as well. "Atomic," "Hydrogen" and "Space" are the successive names given to this age. Our generation has been described by some as the "silent generation," by others as the "beat generation." As Torah Jews, however, we look upon this age and generation as the forerunner of *Geulah*—of Redemption—for we see in all the Divine pattern of the Almighty. Redemption, however, must be earned; it presents a challenge which must be met with wisdom and maturity. What has become increasingly clear is the imperative need for a renewed ascent by all ranks of American Jews to our original source, and a common reaffirmation of our ancient principles.

The Book of Books—the Torah—is being rediscovered. Every book, however, has a *Hakdomah*, an introduction, and our Book is no exception. The introduction to Torah has been taught to us. *Derech Eretz Kodmah L'Torah*—Respect precedes Torah! That is the introduction and we must peruse it most carefully and diligently. Before we can hope to open once again the book that shall guide and direct us, we must study and apply the "Hakdomah," in order to make the teachings of Torah meaningful to our generation.

# Chapter 10

# Patterns of Morality

"We all know that everyone drinks too much. Everyone knows that morality is going down the drain and there's nothing that can be done about it". This quote is from a statement made by a young defendant in a sordid case involving a group of youngsters, all members of affluent families in a well-known, well-to-do community.

This ambivalent expression of defiance and despair seems to echo the sentiment of the younger generation and in turn is elaborated upon in various magazine articles examining the pattern of morality—or the lack of it—in our fair country. Attention has centered in recent years on the "new" moral code evolving on college campuses. There can be no doubt, however, that the college campus reflects conditions in society as a whole. The spirit of these studies of campus behavior and the conclusions drawn therefrom range from outraged condemnation, to resignation, to an inevitable or sophisticated acceptance.

This objectivity and restraint exercised in judging our young people would be quite commendable were the situation not so alarming and dangerous. As Torah-oriented Jews, sexual immorality arouses in us not only indignation but apprehension, for we believe that the erosion of the moral foundations and fibre of a society will prove fatal to the strength, and eventually the existence, of that society.

A disturbing factor revealed in these magazine pieces is the apparent forfeiture of responsibility on the part of parents and college administrations in dealing with the deterioration of moral standards. Some parents and deans have frankly stated that it is not in their province to give direction or exert influence in an area where intelligent, mature individuals must make their own private decisions. This amazing abdication of authority in the dubious name of freedom gives us pause to question just what parents and higher institutions of education are committed to teach. To tolerate laxity in moral behavior through laxity in supervision and control would seem to be highly irresponsible and a debasement of the very ideas to which parents and universities are supposedly dedicated.

As already indicated, the moral revolution, as it has been called by some, or collapse and anarchy, a more suitable term chosen by others, is not the exclusive pursuit of collegians. It is a general condition of our times. The moral posture needs radical correction as it threatens to collapse in a climate of permissiveness, indulgence, and "hefkeruth." An atmosphere of excessive liberty accompanied by a spirit of aimlessness underlines the compelling need for direction, firm purpose, and the exercise of self-control.

Indeed we must examine the devaluation of morals and the vanishing standards of decency in a much broader context. We tend to associate immorality with sexual promiscuity. But what of other areas, for moral standards and ethical behavior go far beyond the narrow confined area of sex. There is the market place, the business and professional arena. Political, fraternal, civic, and religious organizational life have their full share of unethical and immoral behavior. Nor can we ignore the simple, everyday area of human relationship, for in our social contacts there are constant moral issues confronting us and our moral code determines our behavior and conduct in our relationship with family, friends, and neighbors.

There is an urgent need at this point for some definitions. What do we mean by "moral" and "ethical" behavior? "Conforming to generally accepted ideas of what is right and just in human conduct," is the dictionary definition of *moral*—which poses a perplexing problem. Who or what determines what is right and just? Ethics is defined as "ideal conduct and a knowledge of good and evil." This in turn presupposes a fixed, immutable concept of good and evil, which to many is debatable. In essence, what yardstick is to be used in measuring moral and ethical standards? The area of morality and ethics has been described as that "area of human conduct which neither law nor public opinion can really

*Patterns of Morality*

control." A noble and eloquent thought, but here again there is a pre-conception of self-discipline and control which has not been too apparent or popular in recent years.

We are confronted then with an elementary but imperative need: to establish a source of moral authority, universal and timeless, which shall serve as guide and deterrent. A member of the younger generation, echoing no doubt the sentiment of his contemporaries, is quoted as stating, "We are searching, experimenting, and questioning to find our own answers." But if each generation will establish its own code and standard of morality there can be no stability, direction, or purpose worthy of a civilized society. Some of the answers have apparently been found and are as disconcerting as they are debilitating. A progressive professor is most enthusiastic about one of them and he salutes the establishment of a single standard by this generation—equality of the sexes in sex—as a refreshing, honest rejection of the long-practiced and long-accepted double standard. If this be a new modern answer, in all fairness let it be said that Judaism long ago anticipated this attitude. We also have never condoned the double standard and constantly demanded a single one for all—namely, chastity!

The search of the young generation is doubtless a sincere one. It serves but to heighten the urgency of our responsibility in teaching the never-old moral code of Torah. Moral and ethical behavior in every human endeavor is the goal of Judaism—an aspect of Torah which few appreciate. The observance of all mitzvoth is calculated to refine man, the commandment pertaining to Divine Service, *Beyn Odom L'Mokom*, no less than the ethical commandments, *Beyn Odom L'Chavero*.

It is not our intention to further bemoan and bewail the moral collapse of our age. Lamentation is of little value unless it leads to understanding and correction. Historically our lamentation was never the useless "why" but the provoking "how" (*eychah*). The latter question leads to correction and rebuilding while the former is frustrating and futile. We must examine and analyze the desensitized moral spirit of our time and attempt to understand this moral retrogression so that certain concrete suggestions and proposals can be offered.

The search for a "new morality," in our opinion indicates a loss of the old, not its rejection. One cannot reject what one has rarely witnessed or has not even been taught. We have come to a period in our culture where a consistent, honest, properly motivated code of morality is rarely found in our adult society. How then can the younger generation discover its moral bearings? The lack of a moral code and ethical standards is unquestionably due to the fact that values determined by reason, without a superior authority imposing this code upon mankind, is easily rationalized into oblivion. It is folly to expect adherence to a moral code unless there be a fixed, established point, immutable and unquestionable, to which man can relate as the center of his standard of values, and from which radiates the code of behavior guiding his conduct and attitudes. We believe that there can be no moral code springing naturally from the heart of man without a discipline and authority superior to man's own intelligence and inclinations.

Judaism teaches us that man alone cannot establish standards of good and evil without Divine instruction. He cannot formulate a structure of morality through speculative thought. It must be taught to him and related to a concept of holiness. Beyond the good is the holy. This was demonstrated to us at the very beginning of Creation. The first six days are "good," followed by the Sabbath which is "holy." The good life is both formed and guarded by the concept of sanctity.

The Jewish people was given a mission: to be *holy*. They were not admonished to be *good*. Incongruous as this may sound today, holiness is still the Jewish purpose in life. The code of human morality to which the world has adhered in its saner moments derives from what was taught by us. If man has become an ethical infant while growing into a nuclear giant, it is not because he has not found a moral standard but because he has forgotten what he was taught. Much of the guilt, however, lies with the teacher as well as the student. Immorality has always existed, in every society and in every age. So we are told by many who would console us in our hour of crisis. What they fail to appreciate is that today our increased knowledge and added sophistication have brought about a rationalization and justification of immorality. Deviation from accepted norms and departure from traditional values is not even looked upon askance but laboriously explained to us in technical language, giving them an aura of respectability. This is neither surprising nor unexpected. Morality, like nature, abhors a vacuum; the rejection of one set of values must be replaced by another. Negation is not sufficient. The "new morality" becomes a principle promulgated in the name of freedom and liberty. The inviolate rights of the individual are championed, and the evil of a censorship is invoked, whenever attempts are made to curb excesses and establish an elementary code of decency.

Our antidote to this moral retrogression must be a unique, Torah-centered one. Any serious student of the American scene will realize that we cannot combat this erosion through edict but through education, convincing rather than condemning. It is interesting to note that a number of writers have made the observation that there is a need for grace more than for propriety in establishing standards for our younger generation. We would go beyond this and say that not through prudery, but through purity will we be able to establish the moral and ethical values which we are so desperately seeking. Sanctity, not suppression, holiness rather than harassment, is the key to this problem.

Judaism has never been puritanical or prudish. It has ever been practical and candid about sex, placing it in its proper perspective. The Bible, Mishnah, and Talmud are replete with the frankest discussions in this area. What insures the good taste of these passages and laws is the spirit of purity and reverence which imbues every word.

A newspaper ad for a recent "adult movie" proclaimed "Sex is not a dirty word!" Of course it is not! It is movies such as the shoddy one whose lurid wares were advertised by this pungent phrase which have sullied and defiled what Judaism has always dignified and sanctified when properly experienced.

How ironic that art and literature, which were meant to ennoble man and bring culture and dignity to his life, have become the instruments of his vulgarization. In their eagerness to rebel against the "American puritanical spirit," the bearers of contemporary literary and artistic expression have succeeded in spreading a crust of coarseness over the culture of the modern world. This has an increasingly demeaning effect upon daily life in light of the ever-increasing hours of leisure and relaxation, which must be filled somehow.

None of us, unfortunately, is immune to this sex-saturated society. The Torah Jew, together with everyone else, is constantly buffeted and pulverized by his surroundings, and finds it most difficult to withstand the pleasant enticements and blandishments of his environment. The problem therefore is as much ours, as Torah Jews, as it is ours as members of the American society.

When the moral spirit is desensitized most of us are subjected to the tyranny of the commonplace. We live in servitude to public opinion. However, it may very well be that our salvation lies precisely in the banality of immorality. When the immoral becomes commonplace it also becomes a bore and man begins to seek different values and some disciplines as well. The time may well be ripe for a new revolution whereby virtue will suddenly become endowed with vitality and chastity will become the sign of courage. The vital question is, how we can best meet this challenge and opportunity?

The passage of time has in no way diminished certain verities. The development of our character and that of our children still revolves around three major forces—the home, the school, and the synagogue. These three forces must expend a maximum of energy, talent, and resources in coming to grips with the moral climate of our times. It is not too much to hope that as much time, effort, and energy be directed towards creating a proper moral and ethical climate for our communities as is spent in other endeavors to which we seem to be much more sensitive.

A wise man once observed that youngsters need models more than critics. To implant values, a moral code, and ethical standard, the home must create the attitude, set the tone, and establish the norm through example.

Character is not endowed, it is built. The brick and mortar lie in constant conditioning. Chastity, modesty, honesty, and integrity are ephemeral qualities without any real meaning, if they are not constantly practiced. Consistency in every phase of human endeavor, observed in the parents by the child, is still the best teacher. The mode of dress of the mother establishes the pattern for the daughter. The social activities of the parents will set the standard for the children. The language spoken in the household, the ethical element fostered by deeds at home and at business, the ideas and

## Patterns of Morality

ideals exalted by parents, create a conditioning for character and attitude. Judaism has ever taught that restraint within is far more important than restriction without; that preaching is impotent whereas practicing is impressive, and moral action far more effective than moral homilies.

The second force in this program of character-building and creating a healthful moral climate is the school. Whether it be elementary, secondary, or university, the leadership and faculties of educational institutions cannot evade their responsibility or abdicate their duty as educators of young minds and hearts. Yeshivoth have not placed sufficient stress upon character training. How much more so is this true of the secular schools. Knowledge and skills have been imparted with little attention given to molding the ethical will and shaping the moral choice. The dean of a university may understandably be reluctant to impose a moral code of behavior for fear of appearing dogmatic. The dean of a yeshivah has no such impediment, nor any excuse for allowing moral teachings to be relegated at best to brief character-training lectures at infrequent intervals.

The *Mussar* lecture can be of dynamic value and yet is far too rarely utilized. Emphasis can be placed upon ethical and moral values inherent in every aspect of Torah, be it Biblical story, law, or halochah, if our teachers were to be properly oriented thereto and a concerted effort made to incorporate these lessons into curricula. So much attention is given to the development of intelligence, knowledge, and the accumulation of information and data and so little to that of character, ethical behavior, and moral attitude. As important as technical tools is the implanting of good taste, and appreciation of balance, proportion, and symmetry in human relationship. The Torah certainly teaches us all this, but do we spell it out and translate it clearly to our students in our yeshivoth?

In the structure of our society the synagogue-center has come to play an increasingly important role in its contact with people and especially with youngsters. A rare opportunity is being granted to the synagogue and its leadership in molding and shaping the character of present-day young men and women, young boys and girls. The various activities and functions sponsored by the synagogue can be utilized in creating the proper moral climate. The central challenge of our time, perhaps, is to foster a program of activity for teenagers and young adults which would serve to counteract the incessant impingement of immorality upon the consciousness of these young people. Great courage and vision is called for if the synagogue is not to allow itself to become caught up in the very same stream of senseless, meaningless activity in which our culture abounds. The social activities sponsored by a synagogue can set a revolutionary pattern, which would no doubt be at complete divergence with the accepted norm of the street and of society, but which may very well have great appeal precisely because it cannot be found elsewhere.

Lectures, discussions, and symposiums, which come to grips with the moral erosion and collapse of our time, where chastity and modesty would be projected as a pattern of virtues which need not be looked upon as a lack of modernity, would be welcomed. A call for return to an era of grace, sensitivity, and decency—feelings which are not alien to the innermost emotions of teenagers—would strike a responsive chord. The beauty of holiness can be developed and nurtured in young peoples' minds, an appreciation of classical art and music, just as readily as other tastes, and fashions and fads, have been inculcated in them and to which they so slavishly conform.

There is no reason why we cannot cash in on the bankruptcy of the past decades. There is a certain tyranny of conformity from which many young people would gladly escape if there would be offered to them a set of values in which they can believe and which they can practice. If these values would be observed in the adult sphere there is no reason to doubt that it would serve as a source of inspiration to the younger one. Experience has proven that programs of value and worth, properly planned and executed, are enthusiastically accepted by our youth. That they are proud to be identified with a synagogue which sets high standards of morality and insists upon a standard in activities which are absent in other centers, clubs, or organizations. There is a certain prestige involved in being disciplined individuals, as long as the motivation is purity rather than prudery, conviction rather than criticism of others, sanctity rather than suppression.

The moral revolution for which we are searching will be realized only when the home, school, and synagogue will combine their efforts toward the goal of rediscovering the mission of Jewish people which so many of us have forgotten—to be "a kingdom of priests and a holy nation."

There is no doubt that the moral collapse is greatly due to the fact that science has reduced the fear of disease and conception while skepticism has eliminated the fear of retribution. Pure reason, cultured standards of civilized society, even the moral law within man (so dear to the heart of Kant) are ineffective barriers to the constant temptations of a sex-saturated, success-obsessed culture. These are deterrents developed by man himself, which are as weak and vulnerable as he is—as time and history have proven. One is reminded of the wise statement, laced with irony, that if the delights of the next world were visible and the pleasures of this world only imaginary—rather than the reverse—the job of our spiritual leaders would be much easier.

The re-establishment of moral man in a moral universe guided by moral law can be realized only if the authority of law and the sanctions which flow from it are impressed and imprinted upon the mind and soul of man, thereby conditioning his character and affecting his conduct. If this sounds strange and alien to modern man, it must not be rejected by the people entrusted with the historic mission of being a holy people.

True, some of our co-religionists may even be in the forefront of those demanding increased permissiveness and the lowering of the few remaining moral barriers. Witness the two-day demonstrations, a while back, by a few hundred students at Brandeis University protesting a new rule requiring that doors of dormitories be kept open whenever a young lady is visiting a young man. Their cry was that "meaningful relationships between the sexes cannot be established with such restrictions." This attitude must not be permitted to deter us from seeking a revolutionary change. Quite the contrary. Opposition should serve but to heighten the special responsibility of the Torah Jew. Though we be aliens to fashion and strangers to fad we cannot ignore the still, small voice within us which demands that we give genuine grace to our lives.

\* \* \*

Our environment abounds with cynics who know the price of everything and the value of nothing. Responsible leaders in their quest for popularity have been giving candied opinions instead of candid ones. Moral cowardice rather than moral courage is manifested in the most important areas of our society. It is for these reasons that the Torah Jew must learn not to confuse rationalization with reason or theory with truth. We must commit ourselves to the basic principle of our faith that morality is our full-time occupation and must not be used like a bus which we ride only when it is going our way. We have been charged with the great responsibility of teaching our children and our contemporaries that although character may be manifested in great moments it is made in the small ones. It is our historic responsibility to replace conformity with courage and retrogression with resolve, so that the voice of sanity be heard once again and disciplined ideals be stimulated. We who appreciate the value of everything must be willing to pay the price for our convictions.

## Chapter 11

# Ecology and Jewish Theology

New decades have the tendency of closing the chapter on old, tired, talked-out issues while riveting man's attention to other compelling concerns. This does not mean that the old problems are solved, but the passions and prejudices aroused by them are defused, releasing energies and enthusiasm to consider other issues. As we moved from the sixties to the seventies (or from the twenties to the thirties in the Jewish calendar) we found that the Vietnam War faded as *the* central issue of national debate, while a new one was projected to center stage — that of environmental pollution. The quality of our environment, the air we breathe, the water we drink, and the food we eat is no longer the exclusive concern of conservationists or small activist groups, but it merited major attention in President Nixon's first State of the Union address. Ecology — the branch of science concerned with the inter-relationship of organisms and their environments, is "in" and very much a part of our vocabulary.

The link between religion and ecology has been discussed by perceptive observers who correctly understand that since it is man, with his technological progress and power, who has polluted the waters and fouled the air, then the role and position of man must be carefully studied. His values, his power of dominion granted by the Almighty, must be re-examined. The mastery of man over "the fish of the sea and over the fowl of the air and over the cattle and over all the earth" has obvious limitations that are imposed by his sense of responsibility to himself, society, and the future. The crisis of environmental quality, which is the quality of life itself, cannot be considered only as a political and scientific one but is essentially a religious one, for the ultimate solution lies with man's ability to discipline himself — to control his appetite for more and bigger (which alas is not always better) and to impose limits upon his expansion and productivity. This is not only a moral and ethical problem in the religious context but, above all, one of learning how to define man's role here on earth and how to view the world.

Many have written and spoken of this religious element in ecology, stressing invariably the Biblical story of Creation while touching upon many other important areas such as: "this" versus "other" worldliness; individualism and the social order; G-d's involvement and concern for this world; and finally, the population explosion as an integral part of the pollution problem. How does Torah view this entire ecological problem?

The equation by many of the Jewish and Christian religious interpretations of these questions is erroneous and needs to be corrected. It is important to explain the Torah perspective of man, G-d, "this," and "other" worldliness as well as the relationship and responsibility of the individual to the community. Careful examination will reveal that the Jewish view is fundamentally different from that of Christianity and should prove to be of unique interest to those who are sincerely concerned for the quality of the environment. It is also important that we, ourselves, as Torah Jews, become involved and interested in this problem since the environment must concern us not only in the traditional sense of Jews in exile but also in its purest physical sense as well. We must ask ourselves, as responsible individuals, what is the Torah's attitude regarding man's relationship to his physical environment? What can we do to educate ourselves, and those whom we can influence, to correct the injustices perpetrated against society and nature by man, who may well have been motivated by a misdirected application of the role granted to him by G-d as recorded in our Torah.

Let us first examine the role given to Adam by the Almighty when he was created and placed upon earth to "work and keep" the Garden of Eden. Our Sages see the position of man as that of a partner in Creation (Tractate Shabboth 119 and 10; Sanhedrin 7), a creation that is never ending. As such, man has not only the great privilege of partnership with G-d in creativity but an even greater responsibility in his exercise of this creative power. He can be neither neutral nor exploitive, rather he must be productive and protective in his positive use of the power granted to him, for the purpose and end result must be "good" as the creation of G-d is good.

The Torah uses two phrases regarding Adam's mastery over Creation. One is *v'kivshuhu*, to conquer and subdue, while the other is *redu*, to have dominion and mastery over the fish, the fowl, and the animal kingdom. It is interesting to note that after the flood, Noah and his sons are blessed by G-d and assured that their fear and dread will be upon "every animal of the earth, upon every bird of the heavens," but no mention is made of subduing or having dominion. The commandment to be fruitful and multiply is, however, repeated to Noah. What is the meaning of these two key words, *v'kivshuhu* and *redu*? What is basically the difference between them? It is important that we understand the significance of these terms for they go to the very heart of the issue that has been raised by many writers when they discuss the religious implications of environmental pollution, namely that of man's creation in the image of G-d and his right to dominion. This, of course, is interpreted by them to justify man's unlimited power to produce, exploit, and even pollute. Samson Raphael Hirsch, in his commentary on the Torah, interprets the phrase *redu* to mean the bringing down of something from its own free height into the power of another. It was ordained that all living creatures and the earth as well be brought under the sway of man. In this sense the word "dominion" is correct, but only partially so, for as our great commentator Rashi points out, the expression *veyirdu* has a twofold and two edged meaning. One is to have mastery, but the other connotation is to descend. Although he makes this observation in a homiletic sense, it underlines a fundamental point of view as to man's role as master and the limitations of his dominion. As Hirsch stresses, man has not been given the right or the power to have all subservient to him. "The earth and its creatures may have other relationships of which we are ignorant, in which they serve their own purpose." (Bereshith 1,26) In other words, beyond the control of man over nature there is a higher control, a Divine one, whereby G-d's purpose and objective is served and with which man has no right to interfere.

The name Adam is derived from *adomah*, the earth whence he was formed and to which he returns. His dependency as well as his origin is established in his name, even as he is granted mastery. In the Torah view, man must learn to limit his dominion to that of cultivating and developing the earth and its riches in a manner that is consonant with the dual meaning of *veyirdu*, sensitive to the implication that there must be harmony with nature, tempering his drive for mastery. Man must learn to master and control himself, his greed and appetites, even as he controls the world, avoiding the exploitation that is both selfish and senseless. Otherwise he will bring himself down, eventually destroying his environment, and descending to a level that is unlivable, thereby negating the very fruits of his mastery.

The "bringing down" of other creatures from their level of free will under the will and mastery of man, as Hirsch puts it, is meaningful only if man himself is considered to be a being of free will. The Jewish view of man is that he is a free agent and that the meaning of man created in "the image of G-d" is his ability and power to choose, just as G-d has the ultimate power of free choice. One of the names that the Torah applies to the Almighty is Shaddai, which is a contraction of the phrase "that I have said to my world — sufficient" — *she'omarti le'olam dai*. (Chagigah 12; Midrash Rabbah, Bereshith, 10) The cessation of creation, the calling of a halt to the expansion of matter, is a manifestation of G-d's omnipotence. When G-d created the world, our Sages tell us, there was a threat of physical matter getting out of hand. When the Almighty called a halt to the unlimited expansion of matter, He set limits upon the very proliferation of nature and at the same time implanted within man this same capacity. Man has the power, if he has the will, to emulate the ways of G-d; he does so when, upon seeing that his expansion and material growth threatens to overwhelm nature's reserves and the quality of his environment, he calls a halt, voluntarily, to his own creativity and productivity. The stewardship role of man is clearly coupled with the responsibility of man to himself and the world in the Torah perspective for he must be subservient to G-d and His plan, not to society's demands and wants.

The pattern established in the creation of man is not that of a master who can exploit nature's resources but of a partner who will utilize and refine the world's treasures. The meaning of the word *v'kivshuhu* now becomes clearer. Although it does mean to conquer and subdue, it is dependent upon the ability of man to simultaneously suppress and subdue his own selfish desires and greed. The mighty man, the conquerer, has been defined in the Mishnah as one who subdues and conquers his own evil inclination. (Ovoth 4,1)

Hence, the commandment to conquer and subdue the world and all its creatures has its own inherent inhibition and limitation — the suppressing of man's rapacious spirit and his acceptance of responsible restraints. Only man's power of self-discipline can bring these restraints to bear. The fact that the mitzvah of "be fruitful and multiply" precedes *v'kivshuhu* indicates that only if the purpose and ultimate goal of mastery is for the social order, the needs of the family, the development of the home and society, is it granted to man to subdue and conquer nature. The promise that G-d gives to Noah, that the fear of man will be upon the animals and fowl, as well as the granting of the privilege to use and consume them, is also prefaced with the commandment to be fruitful and multiply. This is for the same reason mentioned above, namely, that the power granted to man over the animal kingdom as well as over nature is limited to the positive productive needs of society. Since mankind had, before the Flood, failed to subdue its own evil inclinations and gone beyond its legitimate limits of dominion, the post-Flood generation is no longer granted the power of *kibush* — to conquer, or of *redu* — dominion.

From all that we have presented in the interpretation of the Torah perspective of man and his relationship to the world, we see that mankind was never given the unlimited right to use and abuse the natural resources of the world as its unquestioned and unchallenged master. Just as when G-d created the world He looked upon Creation and proclaimed it to be good, so must man in his role as G-d's partner in the ongoing process of Creation utilize his intelligence, his skills, and his powers to create that which is good. Whatever corrupts and disrupts the harmony of nature is but a manifestation of the words of *Kohelleth*: "Behold G-d has made man straightforward but they have sought out many accountings." When man ceases to exercise his self-control, in failing to call a cessation to his own creativity, then he also fails to choose that which G-d has commanded him to choose, namely, life itself.

"Choose life" (Devorim 30,19) means to choose the ways of life that secure and replenish it, for man must realize that his role is that of sustainer and not that of survivor. Judaism is concerned very much with this world and its quality, the soil, air, and water, and not that of the "other world," which is purely spiritual. Judaism, in other words, does not teach or support the idea of man's limitless dominion and mastery of Creation.

An area of serious consideration, in any discussion of religious thought and ecology, must be that of G-d's transcendance or His involvement and concern with this world. We have already indicated that Judaism views G-d not only as the Creator but also as Master of the universe, hence, His very direct involvement and concern with this world and mankind. Unlike Christian religious thought which often removed the Creator from His creation, once the world was brought into being, Judaism has always stressed the imminence and involvement of G-d not only in this world and in nature but also in history. When the Torah uses the phrase "And the Lord came down to see the city and the tower" or "I will go down" in connection with Sodom, we are being taught in a most emphatic and graphic manner of G-d's ongoing concern for and with the events of man here on earth. The ten plagues visited upon Egypt are a dramatic lesson taught for all time of G-d's mastery over the elements, all living creatures and man, as well as His involvement in the history of a people and the events surrounding its destiny. All this, of course, comes to a crescendo at the Revelation at Sinai when the ultimate *va'yayred* occurs: "And the Lord descended upon Mt. Sinai." (Shemoth 19,20)

The building of the *Mishkon*, the Sanctuary, brought this thought even closer to Israel with the realization that G-d actually was dwelling in their midst. How could such a G-d be detached and remote and removed from their society and this world? The impact made upon the Jewish mind through the Revelation of Torah in a direct manner and the dwelling of G-d in the Sanctuary was then carried beyond the desert into their permanent dwelling place, the Land of Israel.

The centrality of the Land of Israel in Jewish theology is extremely important to an understanding of G-d's relationship to the physical world and the relationship of the Jewish people to nature as well. The statement made recently by a perceptive observer of religion that "it might have been better for the natural order if Baal and other nature gods had triumphed over [*Ha-Shem*] when the Israelites moved into Canaan" is indicative of an unfortunate misconception of the relationship and attitude of the Almighty to the Land of Israel. The Torah tells us that the eyes of G-d are turned to the land of Israel "from the beginning of the year to the end thereof." The three Festivals are agricultural as well as spiritual, in their very nature and essence. The prayers of the Jews for rain and dew have ever been an integral part of their religion. The attitude of the people to the soil was saturated with a sense of sanctity and they attributed magical qualities even to the air when they said "the air of the land of Israel makes one wise." (Baba Bathra 158) It certainly follows that such an attitude of sanctity and reverence would militate against the abuse of natural resources and the pollution of air and water, for it would be not only wasteful but a desecration.

*Goluth*, the exile, has deprived the Jewish people of this sensitivity to land and environment in the physical sense. Dispersed as they were among the nations, Jews have been concerned far more with their social and political environment than with ecology. The return, in recent years, to the Land of Israel has signaled a revival of the traditional Jewish respect for environmental quality as witness the passionate pursuit of draining the swamps, restoring the forest lands, and reclaiming the desert. We see, from a number of ordinances instituted by the Sages in the time of the Mishnah, a profound concern for the quality of the environment and the protection of the quality of living conditions in the land of Israel. "One must keep his tree at a distance of twenty-five cubits away from the town," (Mishnah Baba Bathra 2,7) in order not to interfere with the beauty and amenities of the town. "A permanent threshing floor must be kept at a distance of fifty cubits from a town," (*ibid.* 2,8) because excessive chaff may cause harm to sowers and cause their seed to dry. "Carcasses, graves, and tanneries must be kept at fifty cubits from a town" (*ibid.* 2,9) on account of the obnoxious odors. It is interesting to note that others concur only if the prevailing winds are strong enough to carry the odor to the town.

There are many other Mishnayoth in the same chapter with similar restrictions. Zoning regulations were strictly enforced not only for social reasons and in keeping with good city planning but because they were motivated by a desire to guarantee the quality and sanctity of the land. Our Sages went so far as to prohibit the raising of small cattle in the Land of Israel for they were concerned lest these animals would interfere with the productivity of the land. (Mishnah Baba Kama 7,7) Even the needs of the Holy Temple were not deemed important enough to override the greater need of protecting the natural resources of the land. "All trees are acceptable for the fire on the altar save that of olive trees and vines." (Tomid 2,3) The reason, obviously, was to protect these all-important fruit-bearing trees!

From all the examples cited, we realize that ecology was certainly the concern of the Sages and Jewish authorities when Israel dwelt in it's own land. This concern was motivated by a fundamental reverence for the world at large, which is the handiwork of G-d; the special character of the Land of Israel, which is sacred; and the responsibility of society to insure the safety and comfort of man who is created in the image of G-d.

From the examples cited we can also see that the rights of the individual were subordinated to that of the community. Since in Jewish religious thought the social laws of the Torah and the Talmud are part of a religious code, no less than those that are ritual and ceremonial, we realize that the concept of individualism which characterized much of post-Reformation Christian theology is alien to our theology. To believe, as they did, that salvation is simply a matter between the individual and G-d, and has no connection to his relationship to other persons or the world he lives in, is diametrically opposed to the fundamentals of Judaism. To us, the individual and the community, the *yochid* and the *tzibbur*, are inexorably interwoven and linked. We stress the personal importance of the individual but his position in and with society is even more vital. "And you shall be unto Me a kingdom of priests and a holy nation" is the prelude to the giving of the Ten Commandments. It is not to the individual that Torah was given but to the entire people of Israel. A "kingdom" and a "nation" is the ultimate goal while the individual Jew is but a part of this whole, although retaining his identity and importance.

The individual was given to realize that even his own identity as a Jew, and certainly his fulfillment of the responsibilities placed upon him by G-d when Israel was chosen, can only be retained and strengthened through the k'lal, the community.

Many mitzvoth can be fulfilled only in public. Prayer, the most intimate relationship entered into between man and G-d, requires a minyon, a quorum, for some of its most important and sacred sections in the order of prayer, such as the reading from the Torah and the reciting of the *Kaddish*. The merit of the tzibbur, the congregation, is far greater than that of even the most pious and learned individual. (Ovoth 5,18) G-d is accessible to the community of Israel at all times, whereas to the individual this is true only during the period from Rosh Hashonah to Yom Kippur. (Rosh Hashonah 18) When the individual is judged by G-d, he must possess many *zechuyoth*, merits, and will be deemed guilty in the eyes of Heaven if his transgressions so warrant. The community, on the other hand, although guilty of many transgressions, will be forgiven if unity reigns in their midst and there is a close-knit sense of community responsibility prevailing.\* The mourning laws of the individual are suspended when they coincide with a Yom Tov for he must subordinate his personal emotions and grief to the rejoicing of his people. (Moed Koton 19, Yoreh Deyah 399)

Considering these religious laws and regulations of the individual vis-à-vis the community, we can readily see how Judaism militates against a concept of the individual isolating himself from the community so as to gain his personal salvation. True, he was taught to say of himself "for me the world was created," (Sanhedrin 37) but he also learned that he was vulnerable and desperately needed the "merit of the many." In this sense, the needs of the many were paramount, while the individual's relationship to the community was one of profound responsibility and serious concern. The reason this was so was because the Jew is a member not only of a religious group, but of a nation. He was part of the people of Israel

---

\*Bereshith Rabbah 38, on Hoshea 4, 17: "'Ephraim is joined to idols; let him alone.' Rebbe says: Great is peace that even if worshipping idols and peace is among them so to speak, He cannot dominate over them." Also Ovoth 2,4: "Separate not yourself from the congregation,' and the Zohar's interpretation of the answer of the Shunamith to the question: "Would you be spoken for to the king? . . . I dwell among my own people" (II Kings 4, 13) that it refers to Rosh Hashonah, the "king" meaning "King of the Universe" and her preference to be part of the community when she is judged.

and shared in the inheritance of the Holy Land, therefore, he felt keenly and deeply that the welfare of the people and the land was his. He believed in the dictum "all Israel are responsible one for another." (Shevuoth 39) The spirit of national community was formed by the teachings of Torah, which motivated his life and fashioned his attitude toward the quality of his total environment. This included the society in which he lived and the land in which he had been planted by the Almighty, and as such he accepted the disciplines necessary to insure the health and wellbeing of his fellow man as well as of the natural resources which were a blessing granted to him by the Almighty. The Jew was a partner of the Almighty in creation, as mentioned above, and a partner together with all Israel in developing the land and preserving the quality of the total environment.

This sense of responsibility is still with the religious Jew even in Diaspora where he must transfer his concern to a broader community and to his host land. How erroneous it is, therefore, to equate the Jewish theological approach to ecology with that of the post-Reformation Christian theology which divorces the individual from the community and grants him a kind of religious license to ignore the quality of man's physical environment.

We have attempted to demonstrate that Judaism does not accept the concept of man's unlimited mastery or dominion granted by the Almighty. Judaism does view man as a partner of the Almighty in the process of creation, responsible to G-d and society in his role as preserver and protector of nature's blessings.

It would be well for us traditional Jews to remember our mission to be a light unto the nations and the bearers of G-d's testimony, if we can but penetrate the haze and smog and be seen through the smoke generated by a society that is permeated with a materialistic spirit that pollutes our environment in so many ways. We can help improve the quality of life if we but appreciate the quality of a Torah way of life which can bring a blessing to all.

There are no boundaries in the fight on pollution since there is no way for any community or country to seal itself off from its neighbors. "Universal Man" and "One World" are concepts which became a reality in the realm of ecology. The ultimate solution to this vital problem lies with man, as the original problem was created by man. "We have met the enemy and he is us" is a pithy statement made by a leading American humorist, which indicates incisively both the cause of our trouble as well as the way leading us out of our polluted environment. If it is true, as has once been said, that man can be convinced, woman persuaded, and children distracted, it is also true that we can all be bribed into apathy through avarice or brought to insensitivity through selfishness and greed. The world and its atmosphere will be made safe for man, and all that G-d has created, when men, women, and young people refuse to be bribed and are convinced that pollution control is imperative to their well-being. This will come to pass when they are persuaded that they are partners of the Almighty in the ongoing process of Creation.

## Chapter 12

# "Women's Lib" in Torah Perspective

Judging from the publicity and attention given to the "Women's Liberation" movement during the past few years we must assume that we are confronted with an idea and cause whose time has come, with all the force and power connected with such an idea and its moment in history. "There is naught which has no time" is a dictum of our rabbis, so we ought best take heed. As is so often the case, we as Torah Jews cannot escape this issue, for our Torah and tradition are very much involved. A front page story in a leading daily recently began with a quotation from the Book of Leviticus (Vayikra), citing the chapter dealing with human evaluation (Parshath Archin) to prove that the Bible considers "A woman's effort worth less." To similar effect, a leading exponent of Women's Lib declared in a recent TV program that she first realized the attitude of Judaism toward women when she learned that Jewish men make a blessing each morning "Blessed art Thou . . . Who hath not made me a woman." It is therefore timely to pick up the gauntlet, not to defend but to inform, not to apologize but to enlighten. In an age when the most outrageous theories and ideas are given serious attention, we must not be reluctant to reveal the truth about woman — and man — as seen from the Torah perspective.

At the outset, it is important to define our approach to the role and status of woman. The basic biological differences of men and women with their obvious limiting and fundamental effects are not within the purview of this chapter. We begin where anatomy ends, examining the behavior patterns and personality traits, the natural inclinations and temperament of women, from the perspective of Torah. As such, when we study the story of the creation of woman as related in Bereshith, it is not only the *way* she was created that is

## "Women's Lib" in Torah Perspective

important but the *why* and its implications.

"And G-d said, it is not good that man shall be alone, I shall make a help-meet unto him." Samson R. Hirsch in his monumental commentary on the Torah makes two important comments on this verse. The first refers to the words *lo tov* — "it is not good." In Creation, all that G-d had brought forth is examined by Him and is pronounced to be *tov* — good. Man, however, the crown of G-d's creation, is observed, analyzed, and strangely found to be wanting; he is not complete and the verdict is *lo tov*. Perfection of man, it implies, is possible only if he is not alone; the completion of man is woman. Then and only then can the word *tov* be applied. The second observation Hirsch makes refers to the expression *ezer k'negdo*, a most difficult phrase to translate. The word *ezer* means "a help" but it is also linked to the word *atzor* which denotes limitation, restriction, and confinement. This indicates that the purpose of woman is established from the outset; she is to help by releasing and relieving man from part of his obligations, thereby permitting him to concentrate his efforts in a smaller, more limited sphere of activity which he will now be able to fulfill more completely and to a greater degree of perfection. This help (*ezer*) is not *with* him or *against* him — neither duplicating nor competing but "opposite him," functioning in areas which are uniquely the woman's, "at another point in the same line," in the words of Hirsch. In this manner and with this balance, each of them plays a separate special role while mutually complementing one another.

This concept of equality in diversity of man and woman can also be appreciated in examining the Hebrew terms chosen for them — *iysh* and *ishshah* — so very similar except for the feminine grammatical form. According to one interpretation of the Sages, G-d originally created two faces, male and female, and then separated them, an indication of how they viewed the equality of women.

The method used by the Almighty in creation of woman is most significant. She is taken from man and formed into woman, whereas man himself originated from the earth. It is to this fact that we attribute the earlier spiritual and mental maturity of woman since she was formed out of the feeling, sensitive, living body of man in contrast to Adam whose body was created from earth. When Eve is created her role is well defined. She is not a sex object, or purely a

## "Women's Lib" in Torah Perspective

bearer of children, nor is her purpose only to serve man, tend the children, and keep house. She was to be the ezer, the help-meet, and only through her creation was the original Divine plan of man completed. It is only after the sin of the Tree of Knowledge that her position is altered and she is told "and he shall rule over you." This statement, however, must not be misread. As it is true in the expression regarding man's mastery over nature, so it is here; not an unlimited one but responsible authority exercised with restraint and within bounds. What the Torah is subtly stating is that there is a mystical, almost illogical submission of woman's spirit to man, without relinquishing her role as ezer, and while retaining her unique power of influence and inspiration. The phrase "and he shall rule over you" is preceded by that of "and unto your husband shall your longing be." Not *envy* but *longing*, the desire to be loved, cherished, needed, and even mastered. And so, we see that at the very beginning of time there is established the concept of human beings two yet one, with both similarities and differences, each with a special role to be played in relating to the other and with characteristics unique to each respectively.

Our sages recognized with profound insight the special characteristics of women, their unique personality traits and temperament, as well as their psychological make-up. Many pithy sayings of our rabbis in the Talmud regarding women, their attitudes, emotional complexities, behavior patterns, and predilections, indicate how much importance they attached to the role and position of the woman. Unlike philosophers and thinkers of different ages and of varied cultural and religious background, who either over-idealized women or denigrated them, who over-romanticized or fulminated and fumed at their flightiness and instability, the Sages of the Talmud took an objective, balanced look at woman and reached some interesting conclusions. They found her in many ways superior to man, while in others inferior; they were filled with a mixture of admiration and apprehension and their reactions were as complex and self-contradictory as woman herself. . . . Let us cite a few examples:

"Woman was granted a greater degree of discernment." This does not mean that she was given a stronger sense of intuition but rather an added dimension of perception and understanding, especially in sensing the feeling of others — of being responsive to their emotions. Man is aggressive, while woman is submissive; he destroys and dominates while she heals and re-builds. The ego of man is well developed as is his capacity for selfishness, whereas woman is more capable of selflessness. Because of these differences the Torah also recognized that the attitude of children toward their parents must vary. It is more natural for one to fear his father than his mother, hence the Torah commands us "honor your father and mother," giving priority to the father in the realm of honor, regard, and love, for these are more instinctively accorded to the mother than the father. By the same reasoning the Torah commands one to "fear his mother and father" for reverence, awe, and fear are more naturally given to the father, hence the mother is mentioned first so as to impress upon us the need to revere, not only love, her as well.

As the descendants of Eve, "the mother of all life," woman is committed to life and creativity. This may well be the reason why she is, strangely, not commanded to "be fruitful and multiply," the first Mitzvah given to man! Precisely because this function is part of her very nature and the most basic and powerful force in her life, she needs no such commandment. Man's nature is to conquer, woman's to create. Another interesting reason submitted for the omission of such a cardinal mitzvah from the duties of women, is because childbirth places her in a position of danger to her life and the Torah chooses never to give a direct mitzvah which entails such vulnerability.

Women were praised for refusing to contribute toward the project of the Golden Calf, and lest this be attributed to their parsimonious character, we are reminded that they were more generous than the men when called upon to bring offerings for the Mishkan — the Tabernacle. Their love for Eretz Yisroel was also more profound than that of men ("Women cherish the Land") and they readily and joyfully accepted the Torah.

Another most important characteristic considered by the Sages to be part of woman's nature is that of "tz'niuth," an inherent sense of modesty and shyness. No doubt this is related to her non-aggressive nature, a trait indigenous to the female of the species which even modern-day permissiveness and the liberal climate of our times has not completely destroyed. The expression "her honor is like that of a princess *p'nimah* — within the inner confines of her home," mirrors

## "Women's Lib" in Torah Perspective

the classical Jewish attitude toward women. It reveals not an oppressive, isolated, confined role, so often attributed to Jewish tradition regarding their women, but the tz'niuth associated with her position and her own inclination. One of the most derogatory Talmudic phrases used in criticizing a woman is *yatzonith*, one who "goes out" — implying a woman who leaves the confines of her boundaries and breaks out of the natural, correct borders established by her inherent inclinations. To underscore the importance attached to this virtue by the Sages, suffice it to quote the following: "As the altar, in the sanctuary, atones (for our sins) so does a modest woman in her home (for her family)."

These observations of our Rabbis represent but one side of the coin. The others are frankly uncomplimentary but refreshingly candid. *Nashim daatan kalah aleyhen* — "women are temperamentally lightheaded and flighty" is one of the better known observations to be found in the Talmud. "A woman looks with a grudging eye upon guests," indicates that a man is by nature more hospitable than a woman. Her bent for meddling is revealed in a halachic aside — "A woman is suspected of uncovering the pot of her neighbor to see what she is cooking." The rabbis also recognized her hyper-sensitivity in the phrase "A woman, her tears are frequent" and her need for being humored and patiently dealt with, mirrored in the statement — "Yetzer (the evil inclination), a child, and a woman should be rejected with the left hand while being drawn near with the right."

Above all, our *Chazal* appreciated woman's predilections for extremes. She possesses the inclination to great piety and a powerful devotion to the spiritual. However, she also is weak and vulnerable, more so than man, capable of totally rejecting the spiritual while embracing the secular and material passionately. This trait is obliquely to be found in the Hebrew designations of man and woman. As mentioned above these, though so similar, yet have a subtle and revealing differentiation. Both have a letter of the Divine Name in their designations: man, iysh, the *yod*; woman, ishshah, the *he*. The rabbis tell us that it is most significant that when the letter representing the Almighty is removed, there remains the Hebrew word *eysh*, fire. But it should be noted that in the case of man, fire is composed when G-d's letter, the *yod*, is *removed*,

## "Women's Lib" in Torah Perspective

whereas in that of woman, the fire is always there — G-d's letter, the *he*, must be added to counteract and subdue it! The significance of this is, obviously, that woman more so than man possesses passions that can be consuming and destructive unless controlled, checked, and channeled by faith and piety.

The rabbis were perhaps not as harsh in their assessment of women as a modern critic who, in examining their intellectual delinquencies (as he puts it), was moved to enumerate their deficiencies — "over-statement, tendentious reasoning, lack of humor and subtlety." Nonetheless, the Sages are not overly solicitous in their opinion when they are convinced that certain characteristics should be known and therefore corrected or combatted.

To what extent did the realization of these weaknesses and shortcomings, as well as her virtues and strengths, affect the laws, the mitzvoth, and the halochah regarding women? Although we have a fundamental rule that teaches us that women are exempt from mitzvoth *she-haz'man geromah*, commands that are seasonal and regulated by time, we can nevertheless offer some suggested reasons and explanations for this principle. Especially so if we can find reasons that may mirror the unique psychological make-up of woman. There is a rhythm to the Jewish calendar due not only to the natural seasonal ebb and flow but to the holidays and the rituals associated with them. Samson Raphael Hirsch was most perceptive when he stated that to the Jew the calendar is his catechism. Many of the mitzvoth regulated by time from which women are exempt are related to these holidays. Women have a rhythm of their own which is not dependent upon special times and seasons but is far more regular and consistent. There is in woman's nature a constancy and continuity unaffected by time. This may well be the reason why she in turn is only obligated to fulfill those mitzvoth that are constant. We appreciate the validity of the classical explanation that her household duties make it too difficult for her to accept as many obligations as man. Nonetheless, the suggested reason submitted above may also have merit. It is interesting to note that the negative precepts, the prohibitions of Torah, apply to woman as well as to man because their purpose is to protect and preserve, hence woman is equal to man when the goal is to insure emotional stability and

## "Women's Lib" in Torah Perspective

spiritual health which is the ultimate objective of the negative commands.

It is obvious to any objective student of the Torah and the Talmud that Judaism is deeply concerned for the welfare of women. The Seder Nashim, a special section of the Six Orders of Mishnah, consists of many tractates which attest to this concern; woman's rights and privileges, her financial security and marital rights, the regulations instituted to guard her dignity, and even the aphorisms and epigrams that so often appear in the Talmud, demonstrate the high regard and respect in which woman was held. The areas closed to her, the rights from which she is excluded are not thus restricted out of a spirit of contempt, prejudice, or animosity. They are to be recognized as ordained by the will of the Almighty, Creator of man and woman, Who has prescribed the potential and power of each and their limitations.

In some instances these restrictions are in response to a profound understanding of woman's special role and her difficulty to function in specific areas. For example, her ineligibility to be a witness or judge in a Jewish court is not because her veracity is questioned or her ability to evaluate evidence and reach a decision. The reason is a most interesting and original one. Objectivity is a prime requisite for testifying correctly. Subjectivity is a serious obstacle to the ability of a witness to present proper testimony. Apparently it was felt that the temperament and character of woman is such that her emotional involvement impedes her ability to testify or judge impartially. By her very nature she feels very strongly and partiality is part of her personality, much more so than man.

The expression already mentioned that "women are temperamentally lightheaded and flighty" has aroused the ire of women for centuries and is often quoted to prove the misogynism of the Talmudic Sages. Although it is true that the rabbis meant to indicate in this statement the tendency of women toward superficiality of reasoning, they also meant to teach us in a deeper sense that women are more easily moved than men — prone to exaggerate their emotions, to dramatize their feelings, empathize and identify to such an extent that they cannot retain their objectivity, hence their ineligibility to serve as witness or judge.

The author of the compilation *Torah Temimah* makes a most

interesting distinction between woman's capacity to absorb the fundamentals of knowledge and her ability to reason intuitively and critically. He states that woman's intellectual strength lies in *binah*, the power of discernment — "to understand one thing from another." Her faculty for grasping factual basics, however, is weaker than man's, therefore her superiority in discernment is vitiated and weakened since her foundation of factual knowledge is weak. For this reason woman is not commanded, nor is she really permitted, to study the Oral Law, *Torah She-b'al Peh*, which requires careful structuring and a disciplined process of reasoning which if violated can be dangerous for it would result in a false interpretation of G-d's law.

Although this is a most original and unusual explanation for woman's exemption from the great mitzvah of Talmud Torah, a simpler reason is the concern for her time and her energy being channeled into her duties as wife, mother, and mistress of the household. Torah, to be meaningful, must be mastered and to this end it demands total concentration and commitment, a discipline that Torah did not choose to impose upon woman. For her a different role had been destined. How does Judaism envision this role? What is her status and station in life?

In the early period of Jewish history we find an amazing equality among the patriarchs and matriarchs. In some episodes, such as those of Sarah and Abraham, Rebecca and Isaac, the woman is cast in a far more favorable light and superior position. The same is true of a Miriam, a Deborah, and an Esther in later historical periods. These, of course, are the exceptions, the Biblical heroines, but they also indicate that woman was not automatically relegated to an inferior, secondary role. Realistically, however, the male is considered in Jewish view to be a dominant figure, a *mashpia* (the one who influences) and the female, the *mushpa* (the one who is receptive and influenced).

The blessing recited each morning by every Jewish male, which so disturbed the Women's Lib spokeswoman cited at the beginning of this article, must be properly understood. There is also, as every student of elementary Siddur knows, a blessing recited by the woman — ". . . Who has made me according to His will" — a b'rochah which should not be ignored. The significance of the blessing made by each will be better appreciated if we consider a third b'rochah slightly similar in phraseology. Every morning the Jew recites the blessing "Blessed art Thou O Lord, King of the Universe, Who has not made me a heathen." Now many may not find this great cause for thanksgiving when one considers how much easier and less burdensome it is to be free from all the demands, restrictions, and commandments placed upon a Jew. Yet the Israelite expresses his joy and gratitude for being born into a people that has accepted the yoke of mitzvoth, difficult as it may be. It is in this light that the b'rochah "Who did not make me a woman" is to be understood. It is not a denigration of woman nor a chauvinistic celebration of one's manhood but rather a joyful expression of the added responsibilities and burdens which are incumbent upon a Jewish man. The Jewish woman in turn expresses thankfulness for being a woman, not in the spirit of "I enjoy being a girl" but in appreciation for being chosen by G-d to play a role that only a woman can, fulfilling a purpose and design that is uniquely divine and sacred.

One of the high priestesses of Women's Liberation recently decried woman's existing status as "chattel," the institution of marriage as a crass exchange of the female's services and consortation in return for financial support. She bemoaned "woman exploited by man." This is one popular thesis projected by Women's Lib spokesmen. Others speak, a bit more rationally and persuasively, of the abuse of women's beauty and dignity exploited by hucksters, the entertainment world, and callous men in general. Still others argue that men are assigned to the "human" activities, women to the "animalistic" ones, i.e., bearing and rearing of children, tending to the elementary domestic needs while being excluded from all positions of power and decision in the arenas of commerce, science, and politics. The common denominator is a clamor for freedom from these abuses, liberation from the oppression of women by a chauvinistic male-centered and male-oriented society. Were we to accept these arguments and bitter recriminations then we would have to ask ourselves whether or not the blessing made by women each morning, mentioned above, is truly a blessing or are we asking our women to indulge in an exercise that is both hypocritical and self-deluding?

## "Women's Lib" in Torah Perspective

The answer, as we see it, lies precisely in the very supposition of this rhetorical question. The Torah viewpoint is radically different from that of the shrill defenders of women's rights. Eve was not created to be a breeder but a mate and partner. Woman is not imprisoned in her home performing animalistic or mechanical duties of feeding, cleaning, and servicing but she is the central figure of the home, the *Akereth Ha-bayith*, the mistress of her home.

One of the rabbis of the Talmud goes beyond this concept when he states: "I never called my wife, 'my wife,' but 'my home,'" — for without her there is no *bayith*, no home and no family. Above all, her paramount role is that of teacher and guide. King Solomon, who had sufficient reason (one might say a thousand reasons) to denigrate woman, speaks of "The Torah — the instruction — of your mother," whereas the father's pedagogic role is referred to as "the admonition of your father." Although not commanded to study Torah, her share in the Torah of her husband and children is recognized as being a major one. She is extolled for "waiting for her husband to return home from the house of study and for making her children go to the synagogue to learn Torah." This may perhaps sound overly simple and naive by modern sophisticated standards but let us remember that it succeeded magnificently not only in rearing generations of scholars and pious men and women but also in maintaining outstandingly happy homes and in insuring the continuity of the Jewish people.

Among the many complaints lodged by the spokesmen for Women's Lib, the most legitimate one in our opinion is that modern society has exploited and abused the dignity, charm, appeal, and beauty of women. From the Torah perspective the solution would be a simple and direct one — to re-establish the traditional moral code and strengthen the inherent virtues of modesty and decency of all women. We are convinced that this would prove the greatest barrier and deterrent to the cheapening and demeaning of womanhood. The motto best suited for militant Women Liberationists should be "Combat license to gain true freedom," for our definition of freedom is built into the Hebrew word itself, *cheyruth* — which also means engraved and imprinted, as were the Ten Commandments, on the tablets of law. This teaches us that only he is free who occupies himself with Torah and lives his life in accordance with its spirit. There is no greater oppression and slavery for both men and women than treating them as objects, demeaning their divine dignity as human beings by vulgarizing their inherent purity and decency, especially in their most intimate relationships. Liberation is a most noble cause, if it liberates us from the perverted and debased values of recent years. Ironically, we find that Orwell's phrase "Freedom is Slavery" has become almost a self-fulfilling prophecy among so many "liberated women."

We note that a number of Women's Lib champions are disturbed by Freud. Traditional Jews welcome this point of view for his theories have been magnified out of proportion by the secular humanist camp. The dehumanizing process, the reduction of man to the animal level, the erosion of sexual and moral restraint and discipline which were set into motion by Freud, or more correctly perhaps by exploiters of his theories, sorely needs deflating. Hopefully, this will be a fringe benefit of the Women's Liberation movement, in addition to that of reducing and perhaps even eradicating the use, abuse, and commercialization of women and their beauty by Madison Avenue and Hollywood.

Women's Lib proponents must realize that the bitter harvest which they bemoan and castigate came from the plantings, not of a society rooted in traditional values and motivated by civilized, cultured standards, but by one that has a strange, ambivalent attitude toward women — ranging from adulation and indulgence to animosity and fear. "Momism" is a part of American culture, as is the "little woman" syndrome and mother-in-law humor. The strong, wise wife and timid, foolish husband created by TV situation comedies has also succeeded in disrupting and confusing the male-female roles. There *is* an identity crisis resulting from all this and one gets the feeling that the ancient Egyptian game is being replayed — that of assigning the male role to the women and that of women to men. The balance and harmony built into the nature of the sexes has been disrupted by modern culture, values, and standards. When any balance of nature is tampered with and violated, the resultant disharmony must bring with it discontent, unhappiness, and frustration. When we deny the *ezer k'negdo* concept we become heirs to the unhappy dissatisfied housewife. When we reject the inherent tz'niuth of woman and subject her to the pressures of modern demands, the result is either a frigid, frustrated female or the ultra-sophisticated swinger, both candidates for the psychiatrist's couch. The rites of passage are difficult enough when one must go from adolescence to adulthood, how much more so when pressured to move from a secure identifiable sex role to a unisex one.

Woman needs admiration, concern, respect, and acceptance of her femininity by man. This being so, what is all important is not the *difference* of the sexes which seems to upset the Women's Lib leaders so much, but the *indifference* that modern society has fostered in family life, especially between husband and wife. The rage, anger, and sense of humiliation which many women feel today is quite understandable. The target, however, is unfortunately incorrect. Man is neither the rival nor the enemy, threatening women's true identity and fulfillment. The real enemy and greatest threat to woman's self-respect and fulfillment is the erosion and destruction of her natural G-d-given characteristics and inclinations, namely compassion, modesty, and being an ezer, a helpmate and partner to her man. These are genetic as well as cultural patterns of women which cannot be discarded without jeopardizing her identity and sapping her strength. When divested or diverted from these qualities, she becomes almost a non-person, a vessel that will perforce be filled with the innocuous or the dangerous. Her compassion can be transformed into a passion for any cause, no matter how irrational or violent; her modesty and decency can be so suffocated that she will surpass man in immorality and vulgarity.

Ultimately, women must look beyond the biological, cultural, and social factors which have brought her to her present status and position in today's world. She must learn to appreciate the Divine design of the Almighty in her creation and understand her destiny as envisioned by the Torah and our Sages. When she will attain or recapture the virtues of the traditional "woman of valor" and appreciate her own unique value and worth, she will recognize this design and destiny which is hers alone and be rewarded with the dignity and honor which was ever the badge and lot of the Jewish woman.

## Chapter 13

# The Intermarriage Issue: Crisis and Challenge

Statistics are not always necessarily correct nor do they reflect the true picture of society's problems. Indeed, we have learned over the years to be wary of jumping to conclusions based upon statistics which at times can mislead us rather than pointing the way to proper solutions. Nonetheless, they do serve a purpose, that of focusing our attention upon a problem which is projected into our consciousness in a most direct and dramatic manner. Whether the figure which has been reported recently, that forty percent of Jewish young people who marry in the United States marry out of their faith, is authentic or not, we cannot escape the gravity of this plague of mixed marriages which is of paramount concern to all serious-minded Jews whatever their degree of religious persuasion and commitment.

We may quibble with the accuracy of these figures presented to us by various experts but we cannot argue with the reality of the situation, one that has been experienced or sensed by rabbis and lay leaders throughout the country. We are in the throes of a crisis which affects the strength and vitality of the American Jewish community, if not its survival. When we consider that this matter of mixed marriages spills over from the goluth to Israel, it serves but to compound its seriousness and increase our alarmed concern.

What has brought Jewry to this perilous point? What are the halachic considerations and is there a way out? The patient lies before us, ill and debilitated, but what is the cause, what virus brought about this disease? It is to these questions that we must address ourselves, for although much has been said and written on this painful subject, it is important for us to analyze the root causes, foresee the eventual consequences, and suggest some remedies from

## The Intermarriage Issue: Crisis and Challenge

the Torah point of view.

Let us examine first the source of the prohibition of intermarriage which for so many centuries was accepted by all Jews. For even those who were lax in other observances accepted the stricture against marrying out of the Jewish faith. The Talmud (Kiddushin 68) bases the prohibition of intermarriage with non-Jews upon the *posuk* in the Torah "Neither shall you make marriages with them; you shall not give your daughter unto his son nor shall you take his daughter unto thy son. For he will turn away your son from following Me, that they may serve other gods" (Devorim/Deuteronomy 7:3-4). All Torah authorities, with a single exception, are of the opinion that the marriage with a non-Jew is not a valid one and is inoperative. This means that unless conversion takes place we cannot even consider the couple as married in the eyes of Jewish law. (We stress this point since there are Reform clergymen who perform such mixed marriages and proclaim in public that they are serving the community by granting ecclesiastical sanction to a union which otherwise would be but a civil marriage.) The Rambam (Hilchoth Issurey Biah Chap. 12) is the only one who is of the opinion that there can technically be marriage with a non-Jew which is valid in the sense that they are husband and wife but the one who enters into such a marriage has violated the prohibition of the Torah mentioned above. It is perhaps for this reason that the Rambam finds it necessary to stress the seriousness of this violation in the following words: "This transgression even though it does not carry with it a death penalty to be administered by the court, nonetheless, let it not be treated lightly for there is a greater loss incurred by such a union than even those prohibited relationships which carry with them a more severe punishment. (The reason is) that the offspring of a prohibited union (*aroyoth*) is still considered his son and is included in the k'lal Yisroel even though he is a *mamzer* (an illegitimate child). The son born, however, from a non-Jewish woman is not considered his son as it is written "for he will turn away thy son" which means he will be removed from the community of G-d. This transgression causes one to cleave to the nations (*goyim*) from whom the Almighty has separated us and causes one to desert his people and his G-d" (Ibid, Halochoth 7-8).

Maimonides also refers us to the period of Ezra when the exiles returned from Babylonia and found that many Jews had intermarried during the period of the Babylonian exile. Ezra, who was a most charismatic and powerful leader of his people, was successful in convincing the majority of these men to set aside their non-Jewish wives, and the Elders, together with the people, entered into a solemn covenant to adhere once again to G-d's Torah. Included specifically in their renewed commitment was the pledge "and we shall not give our daughters to the nations who dwell in our midst nor shall we take their daughter for our sons." It is interesting to note that according to the Jerusalem Talmud, the eighty-five Elders who signed this covenant were the men of the Great Assembly of whom it is said that they "returned the crown to its original glory." We see from this moving historical episode that even in this comparatively early period of Jewish history the problem of intermarriage plagued us, but we also can learn that only vigorous, uncompromising religious leadership was able to stem the tide.

From the time of Abraham who refused to allow his son Isaac to marry one of the daughters of Canaan, Jews have resisted intermarriage for a number of reasons. Before the giving of the Torah the objection would perforce not be a halachic one since all were considered to be "children of Noach." The objection, therefore, would be due to the fear that the wrong wife or husband would lack basic *midoth* — personality traits and nobility of character — which would militate against the establishment of a proper home and family. The fear of idolatry was also great and the weakness of Jews in being prone to ape the ways of their neighbors was always recognized, hence the danger of intermarriage. Obviously, before the giving of the Torah, the choice of one's mate would be from within the small family of Abraham's descendants or with those individuals who observed the seven Noachide laws and were of good character. With the giving of the Torah the prohibition was set forth therein as one of the negative commandments. As already observed, although this prohibition is not as severe as some of the other sexual prohibitions, nonetheless, it carried with it a great psychological impact over the ages, especially when Jews found themselves a minority in various lands and were concerned for the perpetuation of their identity as a people.

Over the centuries Jewish history has taught us that in addition to

## The Intermarriage Issue: Crisis and Challenge

the inner strength and self-discipline of Jews in adhering to the Torah commandment against marriage with non-Jews, the many external barriers erected by the non-Jewish world also served to prevent assimilation through intermarriage. We realize that in many countries of our long dispersion the rate of mixed marriages could have been much higher at times when the animosity of the non-Jewish world toward us subsided and there was a lowering of the many walls, both physical and cultural, which separated the Jews from the outside world. Ours is not the first instance in Jewish History where a projection into an open society has undermined our traditional defenses and catapulted us into a world where both the internal disciplines eroded and the external fences have come down. As was true at times in various European and Asiatic societies, the Jewish community is disarmed by the willingness of our "hosts" to embrace and welcome us. There are, however, two major differences between our time and society and those of comparable stages in past eras. One is the extent of the erosion. Never in Diaspora history as today, was so large a portion of the Jewish community divorced from observance of Jewish tenets and Jewishly illiterate. The other is the existence of organized denominational groupings — who have given not only sanction but respectability and legitimacy to the practice of intermarriage.

The advent of the Reform movement with its minimal demands and requirements and its obsession with leveling the barriers between the Jewish and non-Jewish world planted the seeds, the harvest of which we are now experiencing in this country. In an open society where there is a climate of tolerance, and with the emergence of an "ecumenical" spirit in the Christian community, it is most difficult to impress upon young people the passionate opposition to intermarriage which has played so prominent a role in Jewish consciousness over the past thousands of years. Relationships which are entered into between boys and girls in the public school systems, especially between young men and women on the college campus, will often blossom into romantic love against which the arguments of Jewish identity, continuity, and loyalty are quite impotent. Nonetheless, there had always been one major deterrent, namely, the realization that the Jewish community did not accept intermarriage as part of its life style. Even among the non-religious, or those whose religiosity was marginal, there was a lack of acceptance for such a radical step, and certainly awareness of the onus to be incurred within the Jewish community should one's child cross this real though invisible line.

The religious philosophy preached and practiced within the Reform community and especially as articulated by the Reform clergymen gave a new dimension of respectability and what is even more important, legitimacy, to mixed marriages. Many in Reform temple leadership themselves intermarried and even the offspring of Jewish couples were not provided with a strong Jewish home environment, to say the least. By establishing a Jewish version of Protestantism, it became more and more difficult to convince young people whose homes were devoid of Jewish observance that there was anything wrong in marrying a non-Jew — especially when the religious affiliation of the latter was as tenuous as their own. Although many Jewish parents, whose own life style was far removed from the Jewish way of life, objected to the intermarriage of their children, this attitude was looked upon by the younger generation as being intellectually dishonest and atavistic. It is difficult to convince young people that rejecting intermarriage is important and vital to the Jewish people when the counter argument is, "what will be the difference between my home life and that of my parents?"

The past decade with its permissive environment and ambience of openness, where all restrictions and restraints are under attack, has led inexorably, in a widening circle, to *acceptance* of mixed marriages followed by *approval*. This climate of approval has been fostered by opinion makers who have access to the eye and ear of the public. So many Jews in the media who control the communication channels are themselves intermarried and have been able, through TV talk shows, newspaper feature articles, and magazine pieces to create an attitude of normalcy and legitimacy regarding intermarriage. The secularization of Jewish life during the past half century has also been a contributing factor in reducing the resistance to marrying out of one's faith, since that "faith" is non-existent except for a nominal identification or an insubstantial sentimental attachment to one's ancestry.

It is interesting to note that even as the "establishment" and its standards have been rejected with contempt by many of our youth, the American image of love and marriage has been embraced by Jewish young people. Historically, Jews did not idealize romantic love to the extent that the western Christian world had. This was true especially regarding the institution of marriage where family background, character, piety, and consideration of security and scholarship of one's mate were far more important. There was a realistic perception that marriage based on romantic love alone is most vulnerable as it affects its long-range viability. Yet our hard-headed and often cynical young people of today will protest that religious considerations are of small importance when one has fallen in love, which they are convinced will conquer all. This attitude is buttressed by the image projected by famous men and women who feel constrained to constantly proclaim and protest their outstanding success and happiness with non-Jewish spouses. The recent TV series "Bridget Loves Bernie" is one example of how the media attempted to demonstrate the unimportance of religious barriers which crumble and fall gloriously when confronted by "true love."

For many years the organized Reform ministry accepted with only mild discouragement the practice of so many Reform clergymen who were willing to officiate, or co-officiate with a Christian clergyman, at mixed marriage ceremonies. Not until a survey revealed that close to half of their membership was willing to officiate at mixed marriages did the national organization of Reform clergy, the Central Conference of American Rabbis, become alarmed and finally pass a resolution opposing the performance of mixed marriages. In spite of this seemingly strong stand, the C.C.A.R. could not bring itself to go all the way and coupled its opposition with an amendment recognizing that "historically its members have held and continued to hold divergent interpretations of Jewish tradition" which in simple English means that no sanctions will be applied to any Reform officiant who continues to perform mixed marriages. This same spirit of equivocation was manifested by the New York Board of Rabbis when they passed a resolution denying admission to those rabbis conducting mixed marriages but permitted the continued membership of those guilty of this practice, who are presently members. The question is, how effective will these resolutions be in stemming the tide?

## The Intermarriage Issue: Crisis and Challenge

One can also question how effective the resolution on this subject of the Rabbinical Council of America, passed at a recent convention, will be, and how successful its "pressure approach" will prove to be, considering its own ambivalent approach to the non-orthodox ministry. Although many will applaud the vigorous stand taken by the R.C.A. in their determination to compel the removal from leadership in Jewish communal affairs of those who are guilty of this transgression, and their refusal to "sit with rabbis" who participate in mixed marriage ceremonies, it would seem that this commendable stand presents some perplexing questions as well. For many years the Rabbinical Council of America has adhered to a policy of cooperation with the non-orthodox clerical and congregational organizations, arguing that while disagreeing vehemently with the religious philosophy of these groups, the welfare of the American Jewish community is more important than the theological differences which divide us. They have rejected the argument that their membership in mixed groups lends legitimacy to the deviationists. The question therefore arises as to why this particular transgression of sanctioning mixed marriages is considered so abhorrent, that they are willing to abandon their traditional stance and become as militant in this regard as those in the orthodox camp who have for years refused to sit with non-orthodox clergy in such bodies as the New York Board of Rabbis and the Synagogue Council of America. Certainly denial of G-d's existence, rejection of fundamental beliefs such as Torah *Min Hashomayim* (Divine Revelation), personal violation of the Shabboth and other fundamental mitzvoth, are more grave transgressions than that of officiating at mixed marriages where even the participant is but violating a negative commandment! It remains to be seen whether the R.C.A.'s refusal to sit down with such "rabbis" (whose title even they have now put into quotation marks!), or join those who give them honor and "status" will be carried to its logical conclusion: to refuse to join with those who may be innocent of this particular transgression, but are guilty of yet more serious ones!

That spiritual leaders of various persuasions are illogical in their reasoning can also be seen in the arguments used by some Reform figures to justify their officiating at mixed marriages. A number of them have publicly argued that only by performing such ceremonies will they be able to "work with the couple" and have an opportunity to explain Judaism to the non-Jew while holding on to the loyalty of the Jewish partner. This has a strange yet familiar echo of arguments used for so many years by the Reform movement, that by making things easier we will insure retention of Jewish loyalties, be it a shorter service in the vernacular, removal of religious restrictions, or rejection of the mitzvoth as being too antiquated and irrelevant to our times.

History has proven that reduction does not carry with it increased religious fervor or revival of interest and yet we now observe *reducio ad absurdum* where officiating at mixed marriages is supposed to help retain the Jewishness of the Jewish partner! It is interesting that a similar argument was presented recently in a newspaper article by a young Jewish woman who stated that her Jewishness had "intensified and multiplied" since she married her husband who is a non-practicing Roman Catholic. We may well have stumbled upon a new potent weapon for our Jewish survival kit. . . .

Every crisis, however, presents a situation that is dangerous but also carries with it the seeds of opportunity which may blossom into solutions to the problem at hand. The furor surrounding intermarriage has served to awaken and arouse some latent feelings of loyalty among secular Jews who are sincerely concerned for Jewish continuity. While content to live fully in a non-Jewish world, still they identify themselves with Israel and American Jewish activities. For many years they have believed that one can divest himself of most Jewish trappings while retaining basic loyalties to one's people. The statistics of intermarriage, however, have shocked many of these individuals into a realization that something must be done beyond superficial affiliation and identification, which apparently cannot be transmitted as meaningful values to one's children.

Jewish education, for example, may be one of the beneficiaries of the mixed marriage plague. Jewish Federations are being jarred out of their complacency and are considering seriously the need to fund more liberally those Jewish institutions of chinuch which have a better chance of producing young men and women who will adhere to their faith and people. Many who were insensitive to the threats posed by an open society and ecumenical spirit have begun to speak out with vigor and refreshing frankness regarding their opposition to intermarriage. Indeed, it is imperative to create a climate once again of abhorrence and total rejection by the Jewish community of mixed marriages, for only in this manner will Reform clergymen back away from their insistence upon officiating at such ceremonies. Only by such counter-force will more and more young Jewish people realize that the majority of the Jewish community still refuses to grant respectability and legitimacy to marrying out of our faith.

The non-orthodox communities have also been shocked, to a degree, into a position of agonizing self-appraisal and self-recognition. Although the Conservative clergy has been notably less vociferous in their opposition than have the orthodox, still there are indications that they are beginning to feel a degree of doubt as to how closely they can associate themselves with the Reform branch and how intimate their relationship can continue to be in light of the increasing percentage of Reform mentors who are indulging in spiritual genocide. The more traditional minded Reform clergymen, as well as some younger colleagues who are less ashamed of Jewish particularism and the uniqueness of our people, have obviously been propelled into action as reflected in a resolution passed at a recent C.C.A.R. convention, condemning participation in intermarriage ceremonies. Although this is not to be construed as an admission of bankruptcy on their part, hopefully, it may indicate a reassessment of their "derech" and perhaps even a *hirhur teshuvah* — the beginnings of a repentant spirit. They cannot have failed to observe the rampant alienation of so many of their young people who seek religious expression elsewhere, including mystical philosophies and Jesus-oriented groups. The loss of so many through increased intermarriage must have impressed upon the Reform clergy that superficiality without substance, form without content, and affiliation without commitment, have resulted if not in conscious rejection of Judaism then in casual and unconscious defection. It has been said that pretense often hides not evil but emptiness, and perhaps the plague of mixed marriages will cause many in the non-orthodox camp to realize how long so many have lived with the emptiness of a pretended Judaism, which must develop into a more substantial Judaism if the new generation is to be saved. There has been a laceration of the soul within the Jewish community and who knows whether this may not have awakened many to a much-needed confrontation with the truth of Judaism and the Jewish people. As was said in the time of Lincoln, there is an age when people are "destitute of faith but terrified of skepticism," so we may be witnessing a similar spirit in our Jewish community today.

Continuing this theme of "from the strong comes forth honey" (borrowing a phrase from Samson's riddle in the Book of Judges), we may point to a few other areas where the issue of intermarriage is as much a challenge as it is a crisis. We have already mentioned the shifting stance of the liberal orthodox rabbinate in their relationship to the non-orthodox religious community. We detect a more militant spirit on their part, fueled by the intermarriage crisis which they recognize not as an isolated issue but a manifestation of the dangers inherent in non-Torah "Judaism" for which their leadership must be held accountable. The inevitable cooling off of cordiality between themselves and the non-orthodox camp may well bring them closer to the other forces within the orthodox community whose ongoing militancy has created cleavage between themselves, as moderates, and those they consider to be the "right wing." Unity between the various orthodox rabbinical groups will certainly be beneficial to the total Torah community.

We must not permit ourselves to panic and fall into a state of despondency regarding the precarious state of our people in the open society of America and other tolerant, liberal-minded countries. It would seem that there is always one major weapon left in the arsenal of Jewish survival which is not of our making, but is part of the never-changing Goluth. I refer to the attitude of the non-Jewish community itself toward us and how they envision the Jew. During the week that Reform religious mentors were meeting and the newspapers were filled with stories and articles about intermarriage, there appeared another newspaper item which was most ironic. This news item came from London where a leading Jewish merchant had instituted a court action to restrain the Oxford English Dictionary from continuing to present as its secondary definition of "Jew" the following: "A name of reprobation; specifically applied to a grasping or extortionate money lender or usurer; or a trader who drives hard bargains or deals craftily." Incidentally, the plaintiff lost the suit and this definition was retained. Lest we think that American dictionaries are more understanding and concerned for our sensitivities, Webster's Third New International Dictionary carries as a definition for the noun "Jew": "A person believed to drive a hard bargain," and as a verb form: "To cheat by sharp business practice usually taken to be offensive."

With potential "mechutonim" looking upon us in this manner, the inclination to marry outside the Jewish fold will be restrained if not voluntarily, then due to external duress. There will no doubt be some who will marry out of their faith, to be lost to us in most cases. They will have to live with an added dimension of the confusion which plagues modern man in general and their children will sadly lack a firm, definable shape and form. Most Jews, however, will not accept with equanimity, not to speak of approval, the course which these adopt. Even those among us who tend to exonerate mixed marriages will recoil when confronted with the syncretistic absurdities to which mixed couples are moved to resort in the attempt to reconcile the contradictions of their situation. An example is the device adopted by the daughter of a Jewish father and Catholic mother who told an interviewer recently that she had designed a necklace consisting of a silver Star of David superimposed on a cross. . . . The American dream of freedom, equality, and success will never be so enticing as to destroy the greater vision that Jews have always had of themselves as special, unique, historic people. It is doubtful how happy those intermarried couples will be who have "succeeded" in realizing what they envision as the American dream. In the final analysis, success is getting what you want while happiness is wanting what you get.

We have come to a moment in our history where many have gone beyond the historic Jewish outer limits. As a community we have come to the precipice and seen the deep abyss which lies below. Most Jews will pull back and take a hard look at themselves and their future. Then, we prayerfully hope, those who might otherwise have been swept over the brink will hold fast to their roots, rediscover themselves, and eventually recapture the sublime heritage which must be preserved through all time.

# Part III

# Israel

Introduction

# The Dream and the Reality

> "When the Lord returned the captivity of Zion
> we were like unto them that dream." (Psalms 126)

The centrality of the Land of Israel in Jewish religious thought is apparent to all who study the Bible and Talmud. The full flowering of the Jewish people, indeed the fulfillment of all the mitzvoth of the Torah can only be realized in the land given to them by the Almighty as part of His covenant with Abraham. According to the Ramban even those commandments which are not linked to the land are incomplete when observed outside of Eretz Yisroel.

Galut (exile) is abnormal. Jewish survival in a state of abnormalcy has been the paramount challenge confronting world Jewry for the past two thousand years. The Modern Zionist movement envisioned the return to the Land of Israel, coupled with political independence, as the key to Jewish normalcy. This, however, was illusory for it ignored the primacy of the collective character of the Jewish people in a Jewish State which must reflect the divine purpose for which the land was given to us. Until such time, even in Israel, there can be no normalcy as long as the state is a secular one and its goals are limited by national and political considerations. Twenty-eight years of independence in spite of great accomplishments has brought an equal amount of internal frustration and international isolation. Four wars, chronic economic woes, continuing dependence upon the United States and world Jewry, implacable Arab opposition and animosity have resulted in an Israel that is a beleaguered country, which has unfortunately not solved many of the problems that have beset Jewry for the past two thousand years. Nonetheless, it is a beginning and the state has

## The Dream and the Reality

given a new sense of hope and promise to millions of Jews throughout the world. To the believing Jew it is the breaking of the dawn of redemption, dim as it may seem.

The attitude of the traditional oriented Jew toward the State of Israel is an ambivalent one. He considers the establishment of the state as *atchalta d'guelah*, the "beginning of redemption," even with its shortcomings, appreciating its phenomenal achievements and unifying power among world Jewry. He is uneasy with the fact that the majority of his brethren, both in Israel and throughout the world, do not grasp the spiritual dimension of the Holy Land nor understand how to read developments within Israel from the perspective of Jewish history rooted in the eternal truths and vision of Torah.

The following chapters must be placed in proper perspective for they represent to a certain extent a personal odyssey. A Torah Jew must always face up honestly and frankly to the reality of his existence in galut (exile-diaspora) no matter how well adjusted and comfortable he may be in his second homeland. Visits to Israel perforce leave an emotional impact yet one must strive to avoid the trap of illusions or fail to see the forest for the trees. Hence the chapter giving one's observations resulting from a lengthy stay in Israel immediately before the Six-Day War. That war with its historic impact, the unsettled period which followed and the trauma of the Yom Kippur War evoked the thoughts appearing in subsequent chapters of this section. In conclusion there is a summing up, triggered by the recent outrageous acts of a world that has turned its back on Israel, at best, or is determined to destroy her, G-d forbid, at worst. The unifying theme of the chapters in this section is the eternal link of the Jewish people to, and love for, its land and their never ceasing role as "prisoners of hope."

## Chapter 14

# The Reality of *Galut*

*Galut* is not only a state of being, it is also a state of mind. *Galut* is not only a condition and circumstance, it is a way of life, an attitude and a point of view. It is for these reasons that the wise observation was once made that there are three types of *"galuyot"* for a Jew: among the nations, among Jews and within himself. Realistically, however, there are two kinds of *galut*: the harsh, difficult, tragic kind, and the pleasant *"gutter golos,"* smiling, benign and . . . dangerous. For the Jew in *galut* ever is impaled on the horns of a twin dilemma. When physically safe his very essence and survival as a Jew is in jeopardy. When his spiritual fibre is strongest it is usually when his material and human position is weakest. This anomaly, this irregular erratic and absurd state of affairs, demonstrates clearly the unnatural position of the Jew in *galut*, his artificial being as it were, his abnormality as a Jew outside of *Eretz Yisroel*, which is his natural habitat and place of normalcy.

Is American Jewry in *galut*? Of course it is! It may be a "good" *galut* for which we are grateful, but certainly as Jews (as opposed to human beings) we live in an alien environment where we must *create* artificially a Jewish island in a non-Jewish sea, rather than *living* and growing naturally as Jews. We are not, in brief, as we were meant to be, as we were destined to be . . . a kingdom of priests and a holy people in a holy land. Any deviation from this ordained norm, any disruption of this destiny—means *galut*!

Another point. There is a *k'lal Yisroel*. As long as the major part of this *k'lal* is outside of *Eretz Yisroel*, we are in exile. It matters not our degree of suffering, homelessness or lack of freedom. *Eretz Yisroel* in Jewish tradition is not to be measured in the political, social or humanitarian sense. It is all that and much more. In brief—

## The Reality of Galut

if there is no *geulah*, there is *galut*. Here there can be no co-existence. Redemption is the only antidote for *galut* and until it comes in its fullest and authentic sense the disease of exile is very much with us, with all its debilitating effect, be it denial of personal liberty, religious freedom or the subtle caress of assimilation.

We are in *galut*, else we would not constantly in our prayers petition for the return to Zion. Our prayers are not a sham and a mockery. These are sacred and sincere phrases, the profound outpouring of the Jewish *"neshamah"* praying for both Israel's *and* G-d's return to Jerusalem. The honest question may well be when—the time and moment—has it begun and, therefore, must I be a part of it? That is the only reason why the Torah Jew may still choose to remain in exile, but his aspiration and his deep belief is certainly expressed in every word and phrase which speaks of this return. It therefore must follow that his present status is that of a *galut* Jew, and when we tend to forget it there are others, alas, to remind us.

The ideal and the real—this is ever the story of man. We are no exception. The religious Jew believes that he belongs in Israel. This is his ideal. The real may keep him in *galut*, but he does not delude himself into thinking that this is the ideal. Is then his *"L'shanah Habaah B'Yerushalayim"* authentic, or is it hypocrisy? Perhaps this can best be answered with the story told of the Kotzker Rebbe who said to a *chasid*, "Don't be ashamed to call the Almighty 'Tatte-Father', even though He is not yet so. Keep calling Him 'Tatte' until He really becomes your father."

In summation: Jewry outside of Israel is indeed in *galut*. The effects of *galut*, the nature of *galut* may vary but the reality is there. Return to Zion, of both the people and the *Shechinah* is the ultimate hope. As individual Jews and even as individual congregations we are not dependent for our *survival* as Jews upon land, language or *"malkhut."* We would become obsolete only without Torah. But we are destined to *live* a natural, normal life as Jews and realize our true potential as a people—only in *Eretz Yisroel*.

Chapter 15

# Land of Promise, Fulfillment, and Frustration

The old European saying "A guest for a while, sees for a mile," like many epigrams, does not always hold true in real life—especially as applied to an American tourist visiting Israel on a whirlwind trip. The tourist setting of modern hotels, air-conditioned special buses, guided tours, and selected sight-seeing is not necessarily conducive to an insightful, perceptive understanding of a land, its people, and its problems. If, however, one is able to spend a few months in the Holy Land, living, more or less, as a regular Jerusalemite, and experiencing the daily normal activity of an inhabitant, then the possibility of gaining an understanding and appreciation of Israel is far more feasible. I was fortunate to have been afforded such an opportunity and by absorbing, observing, and above all, listening, was in position to gauge the temper and tempo of the times in the land of our Fathers. Although not claiming to see a mile, nonetheless it is my feeling that I was able to see a kilometer—using Israeli standards.

In a land of such varied topography and ever changing scenery as Israel, where within a single day one can travel from mountain to valley to seashore, from lush green land to desert, variation and contrast are in the natural order of things. And nowadays the diversity of Israel's populace fully equals, and perhaps surpasses, the variety of its physical scene. Coming as they do, from so many different countries with disparity of background and divergent points of view, the population is extremely heterogeneous. Their differences are not easily overcome and certain tensions and conflicts are felt in many facets of society—political, cultural, and above all in social life. All this being so in areas which lend themselves to eventual compromise and solution, how much more so is it in the

## Land of Promise, Fulfillment, and Frustration

area of religious practice and observance.

One could discuss at great length the problems of the political arena, the enigmas of an emerging society, and the tension and strife between conflicting elements of this new community in Israel. We will, however, direct our attention to three areas which are often discussed but deserve more thoughtful and thorough examination. These are areas which affect not only the religious community in Israel and abroad, but which perforce have impact upon the totality of k'lal Yisroel. One of the great deterrents to a proper understanding of the Israeli community today, is the tendency to isolate problems of religion and quarantine them from the mainstream of the Jewish community. We shall attempt here to relate each of these challenging problems to the total picture of Israel—the State and the Nation.

The three areas are: the condition of the religious community in Israel, its composition and leadership—and its perplexities. Secondly, the relationship of the Torah community to the non- and anti-religious elements, with emphasis upon the lines of communication between the *dati* and secular society. Finally, we will analyze the attitude of the Israeli toward the American Jewish community—with some suggestions as to strengthening our ties with Israel and above all enlightening our brethren there.

There is a tendency to evaluate the strength of any given community, quantitatively, using the yardstick of numbers and relying heavily upon statistics. The numbers of synagogues, students in religious schools, and votes for religious-oriented parties in national elections are the normal means by which most observers judge the strength and vigor of the Torah community in Israel. Although these are important elements and can certainly be utilized as criteria of potency and influence, nonetheless there are other, perhaps more accurate ways of evaluating the strength and position of the Israeli religious community.

One cannot spend time in Israel without sensing the vibrancy and extent of Torah living regardless of the city or community in which you choose to spend your days or weeks. The number of schools is increasing, a sense of lively participation in Torah activities is apparent and above all the involvement on the part of youth is obvious. There is no hesitancy on the part of the younger generation to identify themselves with religious forces. The climate is certainly conducive to Torah loyalty and even the opposition to Torah observance serves to spur on its adherents lending added spice and vigor to their allegiance and loyalty. A member of the K'nesseth was most candid in confiding to me that whereas years ago when he delivered fiery speeches in the K'nesseth affirming his faith in the future of Torah Jewry, he himself was plagued by self-doubt. The opposition had almost convinced him that the future belonged to the non-Torah forces and the new generation would certainly abandon the disciplines and demands placed upon them by orthodoxy. Today, however, when he delivers similar talks, he does so with firmness and certitude buttressed by the fact that so many of the new generation have retained their loyalty to the Torah cause while the offspring of the secular-oriented parties have turned their back on the ideas and ideals which were so precious and meaningful to their pioneering fathers. The lament, heard in non-Torah intellectual circles far more than that of Torah circles, is that the youth of the country has lost its bearings, and obscured its goals, thus channeling its energies toward material comfort and financial success.

The bright side of this picture should nevertheless not blind us to the many problems which beset the religious community in Israel today. It would be incorrect, for example, to assume that there is an authoritative voice of Torah in Israel accepted by the observant and respected by the non-observant. It also would be fallacious to give the impression that there is an upsurge of religiosity in the land and a wave of return to the sources of Judaism. The interest in Torah works and the lessening of hostility toward the traditionalists does not mean a spirit of *teshuvah* has appeared. Rather it is indicative of an unrest and ennui which has, as yet, not found a way, goal, or objective.

Within the religious community itself the by-now well-known dichotomy between the yeshivah world and the synagogue, the b'ney Torah and the lay community, is very real and at times quite acute. In Israel, it is perhaps even more radical than here in the United States. The number of yeshivoth is greater, as are the number of young men at the kollelim and their attitude toward the larger religious community is one of suspicion and antagonism since they identify them with political compromises, self-interest, and cupidity. The Rabbinate is unfortunately largely impotent and incapable of exercising the strong leadership which might bridge this gap between the products of the higher yeshivoth and the majority of the religious community.

A word at this point regarding the position of the rabbinate in Israel. Although in some ways the authority and power of the rabbinate is far greater than that of the rabbinate in galuth, since it has state sanction and support, nonetheless this same source of support and sustenance is the seed of its weakness, as well. The rabbi in most instances is considered and functions as a religious officer of the state. He is a religious functionary. He performs weddings, officiates at funerals, and participates in certain simchoth. He does not, however, guide or lead and at times does not even teach or instruct. Too many Israeli rabbis are dependent upon other sources of income, in order to subsist, and although serving officially as rabbis of neighborhoods, are not involved with their people except in a peripheral fashion. Communication with the shul Jew is meager and contact with the non-religious element is reduced to those infrequent moments of life when a rabbi must perforce be used. In our history as a people we were privileged to enjoy strong and meaningful rabbinic leadership when rabbis were chosen to serve and lead the community at large. In modern society this fruitful and meaningful leadership is to be found even where a rabbi is chosen only to serve and lead a given congregation. It is unfortunate that in Israel, where the rabbi is appointed with the consent and backing of the State through the instrument of the Ministry of Religion and the sanction of the Chief Rabbinate, that his role as leader, teacher, and man of influence has become so weakened and debilitated.

This enervation of the rabbinate is not to be attributed completely to the mechanics of appointment and the entire structure of a state-supported clergy. The position and power of the rabbi is shaped by the layman and the role he plays in the community. Unfortunately, the vast majority of religious laymen in Israel show no tendency to exercise responsible leadership in religious communal fields. To a great extent this is due to the fact that there is no great need to exert oneself and invest time, money, and energy in the establishment of religious institutions—be they synagogue or school. Ironically, the assistance lent by the government in obtaining land, building synagogues, and in building and maintaining schools has drained the initiative and sense of self-dedication on the part of baaley-battim, who under other circumstances must give so much of themselves in order to build these institutions and organizations. The special relationship and responsibility created when baaley-battim retain the services of a rabbi for their congregation and community is also woefully lacking in Israel since the rabbi, as already mentioned, is an officer of the state and assigned to the community. Although it is true that the community accepts him upon themselves as their rabbi, nonetheless that special relationship and rapport is lacking. In general, the prestige and status of the rabbinate is not as high or revered as it is in the United States.

To cite a glaring example of the deplorable state of the rabbinate in Israel, one need only point to the almost incomprehensible fact that the Yeshurun Synagogue in Jerusalem, one of the largest and most prestigious synagogues in the land does not have a rabbi: to appreciate the incongruity of this lack, picture if you will, *l'havdil*, St. Patrick's Cathedral minus a priest or bishop. It is interesting to note that when I asked two leading members of this synagogue, one an official in the Ministry of Religion and the other a former New York rabbi, to explain this strange situation—the former was a bit embarrassed while the latter reassured me that at every bar mitzvah either he or some other rabbi does the honors. . . .

The large number of small *shtibelach* and *battey medrash*—ranging from Mizrachi to Chassidic and Neturey Karta orientation—also militates against any influential and strong rabbinate and certainly does not help to foster knowledgeable and responsible laymen. What must be stressed is that the entire condition of the rabbinate and the sad situation of the synagogues does not encourage incipient rabbis to pursue this profession. The only hope for a degree of dignity and status in the future will be a radical retooling of the synagogue structure and of the institution of the rabbinate.

To conclude our observation in this area, let us but relate a little incident of a man who after many years of alienation from Yiddishkeit decided to return to the Synagogue. Shocking as it may sound, this resident of Jerusalem, a serious and sincere man, after exploring and visiting many houses of worship in Jerusalem, came to the sad conclusion that he had "no place to daven." This may be an extreme case but nonetheless should give us pause for reflection and re-examination of the ways and means to reach out and attract many Jews in the State of Israel who would welcome a synagogue and a rabbinate within the framework of Torah—true Judaism, which can reach and touch their Jewish hearts and souls.

The relationship between the religious and the secular communities is most aggravated and a source of sincere concern. Tension and strife gives way at times to cautious watchfulness and controlled restraint, but nonetheless the undercurrent is there. In recent years the more flagrant antireligious attitudes have subsided, flaring up from time to time, when an exposed nerve is touched, such as the recent autopsy question and the ever recurrent Shabboth public transportation issue. What is of paramount importance is that we must appreciate that opportunities now present themselves to challenge the imagination of the non-religious and even gain their admiration and respect for Torah principles and beliefs. When one speaks to the average young non-religious individual he will find not necessarily an antagonism to orthodoxy but an abysmal ignorance and distorted idea of what Torah is and teaches. One must not be misled by the knowledge of the average Israeli, who speaks Hebrew, knows all the expressions, is aware of all the holidays and customs. Yet, he has so often a completely incorrect understanding of the basics of Judaism and certainly of Torah *hashkofah*. To dispel these misconceptions is our greatest task and mission.

An amazingly large number of Israeli youth identify and equate religion with naught but restrictions and restraints—many of which do not even exist. They bring to mind the remark of the octogenarian who said he had lived many years and seen much trouble, much of which never happened. To them, the image of orthodoxy has been presented as a condition of life that is stultifying and suffocating. They have also become antagonistic, because they are convinced that the religious community is imposing its will upon the total community. They are convinced that political maneuvering and trading have resulted in the passing of legislation which has no meaning or significance to them and is not effective—since there is no true motivation on the part of the populace to adhere to these laws—such as Sabbath observance, kashruth and even the marriage and divorce laws.

It is not difficult to understand these complaints. We in this country have learned that it is nigh impossible to superimpose disciplines and restraints where there is no firmly founded deterrent or motivation based upon education, knowledge, and commitment. Above all, if there is a lack of respect combined with a degree of fear, the promise and hope of regaining this element, which is not necessarily non- or anti-religious but rather neutral and confused, is quite weak. Without judging the virtues or shortcomings of the religious political parties, it is a fact that much of the violent opposition to religion per se is tied in with opposition to the religious party as a political force. Much of the opposition, for example, to religious schools in new settlements is not based upon ideological hostility to religious training of immigrant children. It rises rather from concern that religiously trained youngsters may grow up to be potential voters for religious political parties. It is this power struggle that unfortunately hinders and obstructs the possibility of bringing many Jews closer to an understanding of Torah values, unbeclouded by political considerations.

The present situation in Israel is marked by an atmosphere of frustration and spiritual emptiness. There prevails among large elements of the populace a sense of dissatisfaction and non-fulfillment which will either be channeled into a materialistic direction or can be capitalized upon to create a positive and sympathetic attitude toward authentic Jewish values. Since there is so much in the environment of Yiddishkeit, folkways and customs, which are absorbed almost through osmosis, a well-planned and properly organized program of public education and enlightenment has maximum prospect of success. In dispelling the distortion of orthodox Jewry's image and replacing it with an attractive and magnetic one, many could be won over to the Torah ranks.

Without emasculating the religious parties, which in the opinion of this writer have accomplished much through legislation and in their activities in the political arena for the benefit of Torah Judaism, there is room in Israel today for a non-political religious force which could reach out and attract a large element of the non-committed. Many of the activities sponsored by American synagogues and developed by the American rabbinate could be effective in Israel. Once the rabbinate and political religious leadership in Israel could overcome its prejudices and self-interests and cease to place so much stress on external garb and appearance, the American rabbinate and intelligent laity could be of great help and assistance in demonstrating how to reach people and capture them for Torah.

At this point, let us direct our attention to the attitude of Israelis to the American Jewish community in general, and the many misconceptions under which both the religious and non-religious communities labor. Religious Jewry in Israel, with few exceptions, has a distorted picture and image of the American Jewish community. They have conjured up a picture of fully or partially assimilated Jews while even those who may have remained loyal to the faith of their fathers are woefully unlettered and untutored, Jewishly speaking. To be quite blunt about it, the American Jewish community represents to them a reservoir of affluence and prosperity, fortunately generous with their wealth, but as far as Yiddishkeit is concerned, they are either *sh'kutzim* or *ammey hooretz*.

The secular-oriented Israeli, uninterested as he is in the religiosity of his American brethren, still has in common with his orthodox Israeli neighbor a distorted and oblique image of American Jewry. His contact is primarily with tourists and American relatives and he is convinced that we are simple, naive, ingenuous, with a residue of idealism still operative and fortunately a great love for the Land of Israel. They imitate what they consider to be American culture (movies, songs, dances, fashions, and styles) without really admiring it, and their knowledge of the American Jewish community — its problems, promise and progress — is unknown among them. The common denominator of most Israelis in regard to understanding of American Jewry is a view both negative and absurd. There is crying need for clarification and education in this vital area of mutual recognition between the American and Israeli communities. It is ironic and almost paradoxical that in American schools — be they yeshivoth or Talmud Torahs, or even Sunday Schools — substantial time, effort, and energy are expended in teaching our youngsters everything possible about Israel—the land, its people, its history, and its current problems. This is as it should be. Would it not however be equally important, and certainly equitable, to reciprocate in Israeli schools by teaching the children something of the history, development, problems and progress of the largest Jewish community in the world today—the American Jewish community? Not only in our school system is such stress placed upon Israel, but also in our adult programming. Our writings, our sermons, and our lecture platforms alike concentrate much attention upon Israel. It would be most advantageous for Israelis to be exposed to us, through similar media, so as to become acquainted with the American Jewish community. Although there are occasions when Americans are given the opportunity to present themselves to the Israeli public from lecture platforms, at school assemblies and the medium of newspaper interviews, they are far too infrequent and inadequate to present a complete picture of the U.S. Jewry to the Israeli public.

Torah forces in Israel would certainly find it to their advantage to know and understand us as we really are. Would it not be a source of great satisfaction and, more important, would it not strengthen their own morale, for them to know that there is a strong, vibrant, and viable orthodox Jewish community in America? Would it not be to their good to realize that, though modern-garbed, economically successful, and an integral part of America, yet this is a community deeply observant and totally committed to Torah ideals and way of life? Would it not, further, strengthen their own position for this fact to be brought home to Israelis at large? Although one suspects, it may be a bit shocking and ego-deflating for the Israeli to recognize and admit it, it would be good for their souls and encouraging to their morale to realize that there are flourishing yeshivoth in America, thousands of *b'ney torah* and many *lomdim* among its rabbis.

This writer came to realize that it was difficult for many Israelis to differentiate between the various denominations which exist in our midst, thereby causing them to reach an oversimplified conclusion. Since the Orthodox, Conservative and Reform clergymen are seen by them alike, unbearded and in modern garb, and since in most cases conversations revolve around prosaic and non-Torah topics, they are convinced that the American Jewish spiritual leader is a "Rabbiner"—intelligent, personable, competent, successful, and a very limited scholar whose piety is also suspect. It is difficult for the Israeli to appreciate the vast difference in belief and *yirath-shomayim*, let alone scholarship, between the orthodox rabbi and his deviationist counterparts. An intelligent instructor at one of the leading yeshivoth in Jerusalem, who has lived in Israel for the past forty years, had occasion to spend a few pleasant hours at a private kiddush with a young American orthodox rabbi. After exchanging a number of *divrey torah* and discussing various present-day Torah problems, he exclaimed "I never knew that a young American rabbi *zul kenen lehrenen.*" Another Jerusalemite, who is the head of a fine Talmud Torah (here, it would be called a Yeshivah Katanah) asked the writer whether he spoke to his congregation or conducted any classes. He was most interested in knowing whether a sermon could include a quotation from the Torah and whether the audience could understand or appreciate it if the rabbi would be so bold as to include it in his remarks. He found it quite difficult to believe that an American congregation could consist of men who are well versed in Torah, highly appreciative of profound *divrey torah* and who attend Talmud *sh'urim* grasping the intricacies of the *daf* and all the commentaries.

One example of the Israeli's abysmal ignorance of our American Jewish community was manifested very recently when the head of a well-known yeshivah in Tel Aviv remarked that he had heard of two yeshivoth in the United States — Lakewood and Telz. He found it difficult to believe, when so informed, that there were many more great yeshivoth in our country where thousands of young men study Torah and observe the mitzvoth with fervor equal to that of Israelis. These examples and episodes are cited to indicate how uninformed and misinformed are individuals, not of the masses, but men in educational fields, who should certainly know better. One gets the feeling at times that there is an iron curtain between us. What is even more disquieting is the feeling that they do not *want* to know. It is imperative that we exert our efforts in enlightening our Israeli brethren and in supplying them with data and information that they in turn can use to elucidate and educate the Torah community in the Holy Land.

The enlightenment of the Israeli public in understanding the true story of American Jewry would serve not only to strengthen the spirit and sense of optimism of the religious Yishuv, but it also would have a wholesome, salutary effect upon the secular community. Many American visitors to Israel find that their non-religious relatives in the Holy Land are amazed to learn that the well dressed, well educated young man and the chic young lady are American cousins who observe the Torah, send their children to yeshivoth and are sincerely committed to the Torah way of life. This revealing lesson is helpful in altering their distorted concepts and attitudes toward Torah Jewry. How much more so would this be true if a concerted campaign would be instituted to acquaint the entire yishuv with the exciting and inspiring story of American orthodoxy during the past few decades?

We have attempted to show that there is much to be done and gained in establishing a two-way street of communication between ourselves and Israel, in revealing our religious posture and the effect of this revelation upon the Israeli community. There also is much that we can share with them, equal in importance to our financial assistance, which they so readily accept and gratefully acknowledge. One could be so bold as to submit that the future of the Israeli religious community depends upon how well they will understand the paramount role *we* have to play in the Holy Land.

The three areas we have discussed have one thing in common—the need for a well-organized, imaginative program approach which will reach out and strengthen the religious forces in Israel and project a true image of Torah values which will capture the hearts and minds of the vast non-committed Israelis. We have been successful to a substantial degree in doing precisely that on the American scene and can be extremely helpful in the land of our fathers as well.

The American orthodox rabbinate has demonstrated its effectiveness and proven its leadership qualities. The Israeli rabbinate has as yet not done so. The American synagogue has manifested its strength and accomplishments—the Israeli synagogue has yet to do so. The American orthodox yeshivah graduate and Torah-trained young generation has demonstrated how one can live in the modern world successfully while retaining all Jewish teachings and observing the principles of Torah. The Israelis have yet to demonstrate this in equal proportion to our experience.

## Land of Promise, Fulfillment, and Frustration

For all these reasons it is imperative that we impress upon the Israelis, and especially in Torah circles, that an exchange program which is meaningful be instituted whereby Americans who are knowledgeable be invited to spend time in Israel so as to acquaint them with the true picture of the American Jewish community. The rabbinate especially should be asked to share their vast experience with the Israeli rabbinate and not be merely tolerated and looked to as a source of financial support for Israeli institutions and yeshivoth which may well repeat the errors of the past without attempting to solve the problems of the present.

We appreciate that the Israelis have their *taines*, grievances, complaints, and criticisms regarding us. They sincerely feel we are not in a position to advise and guide them. We, in turn, feel that we have much to share with them. Churchill once said to Lord Beaverbrook, the newspaper tycoon, that one or the other of them had always been right, since they had always disagreed. This wry witticism is not necessarily apropos, insofar as "we" and "they" are concerned. There may be a time when both are wrong or when both are right, and areas of agreement can be found. The important factor to remember and never disregard is that we are all part of the same k'lal Yisroel, responsible for and to one another. Our plea and program is simply to institute a two-way street which will include not only tourists and visitors but ideas and experiences as well.

Mutual respect and regard will serve to establish a meaningful dialogue which will in turn be beneficial in promoting western aliyah—the prime guarantee of Israel's future.

Our affection and love for the Land of Israel was not diminished as a result of our added depth of understanding, perception and insight—the fruits of a lengthy stay in the Holy Land. If anything, our love of Eretz Yisroel was increased. It is wise to remember, that while love is the end of indifference, it is also acknowledgement of differences. The two are not mutually exclusive; they are complementary. We recognize the differences of the American and Israeli communities. We shall never, however, become indifferent for Israel is our land, its people our people and their destiny is ours as well. The frustrations will, with G-d's help and our sincerity and wisdom, be transformed into fulfillment—as befits a Promised Land.

Chapter 16

# Days of Trial, Triumph, and Awe

One finds it most difficult to recall a period of Jewish history which so moved and aroused the passions and prayers, the feelings and emotions of our people as did the Six-Day War. Rarely, if ever, have Jews of every religious and political persuasion throughout the world been so intensely involved in the destiny of Eretz Yisroel and her people, so deeply and painfully concerned for her welfare and security, so profoundly identified with her hours of trial and triumph. For a brief period World Jewry experienced anguish and apprehension followed by exhilaration and joy, tempered with a sense of awe and thanksgiving, in the aftermath of victory.

Events developed so rapidly, yet in retrospect, we perceive a preordained pattern of inexorable sequence. The plot unfolded with a degree of exact precision—all pieces falling into place—only the pace changing from the ponderous rhythm of the diplomatic field to the acceleration and lightning crescendo of the battlefield. Through the flashes of lightning, one could perceive the interposition of a Divine plan and pattern—seen not only by the faithful but even by the secular-oriented sophisticates and cynics. The Israeli press was replete—as were private communications from Israel—with the realization that a veritable miracle was occurring, one which, if not as open and obvious as those in the deliverance from Egypt—was as permeating and subtle—and as real—as the *ness* of Purim.

Although we accept without question every aphorism of our Sages there is one that, happily, was momentarily abrogated: "The recipient of the miracle does not recognize the miracle." This may have held true often in our days—including at the founding of the State of Israel—but in Sivan 5727 we redeemed ourselves; we recognized, reacted, and rejoiced in the miracle of Jewish victory and valor. The Se'fath Emeth points out the similarity in the Hebrew language of the word "miracle" (*ness*) to the one signifying "trial" or "test" (*nisayon*). The greatest test is usually the appreciation and awareness that a miracle is occurring—a test rarely passed. Perhaps one of the greatest wonders is that we were equal even to this trial and recognized the "ness"—as it was happening! Why? One major reason may be that we were prepared—and preparation is all-important in creating an atmosphere wherein the ear is sensitive, the eye perceptive, and the heart wise enough to see and understand with clarity what is unfolding. We know how much importance our Sages attached to *hachonah*—preparation—in connection with mitzvoth. We now can appreciate how wise and insightful they were, for "From my own flesh I perceive"—as Job so well phrased it—from one's own "flesh," one's own experience, one sees the profound truth and wisdom of G-d's ways and teachings. We were prepared in the sense that we were so intensely aware of the march of events, which seemed to proceed like chessmen moving on a board, manipulated by unseen players—each move part of a pattern, fitting methodically into the overall picture, each playing out its predestined role. The threatening Arab world, the indecision of the Western powers, the impotence of the U.N., the cynical Communist world—all was enacted before our eyes—seen, recorded, and communicated to us instantly. The newspaper articles of analysis, the commentaries, interviews, and predictions all helped fill in the background for the climactic, explosive events yet to come. We were prepared—as Jews—emotionally and psychologically more so than in '48 and '56—and that is why we reacted with such fervor and passion—why we were so united and generous.

There were other factors differentiating the War of Independence in '48 and the Sinai Campaign of '56 from the electrifying events of June '67.

The termination of the British Mandate, the partition plan of the U.N., and the proclamation of the independent State of Israel, followed by the attack of the Arabs upon the fledgling Jewish State, came in the aftermath of the European destruction and holocaust. World Jewry was still mentally and emotionally overwhelmed by this traumatic experience of evil. Lacerated in every fibre, reeling

## Days of Trial, Triumph, and Awe

before the stupefying enormity of the horror that had transpired before, there now came upon us the epochal, stormy birth of the Jewish State in the Land of Israel. From our farthest depths there was evoked an intensity and passion that took new toll of strained minds and exhausted emotions. So shaken and beset, we were ill prepared to rally our forces with the same instant responsiveness and self-command that has marked this most recent threat to Israel's existence. The sheer incredibility of a Jewish state as a fact in itself made it more difficult to react with a full measure of maturity and responsibility. One found it difficult to grasp the very idea of the existence of a Jewish State; indeed we were gripped by a sense of unreality.

In '56 the suddenness of the Sinai campaign caught us unaware. Coupled with this lack of emotional preparedness was the confusion experienced by American Jews due to the implacable opposition of the United States and in general a sense of disquiet resulting from the awkward coincidence of Israel's move into Sinai with the Anglo-French campaign to recover the Suez Canal. The difficulty of identification with a preventive war was another factor, as was a certain coolness to the idea of battling Nasser over the nationalization of the Suez Canal. The fruits of that victory—access to the Straits of Tiran, U.N. patroling of the Gaza Strip and the defusing of the explosive borders—were not appreciated until later.

The events of 5727/1967, however, had all the elements lacking in 5708/1948 and 5717/1956. There was the anguish of apprehension and anticipation, the sense of fear and frustration, and above all the profound feeling of an Israel—alone! The world was standing by, seemingly helpless and mute in the face of bombastic pronouncements and threats of a new Hitler. The great powers were demonstrating how nuclear giants could be ethical infants; the U.N. was exercising more duplicity than diplomacy with an inadequacy bordering on insolvency, and the menacing spirit of Munich was in the air. To Jews in whose souls were seared the scars of Nazidom, to whom the State of Israel was a vital measure of Divine comfort for the destruction of six million, to whom its inhabitants represented the remnant of European Jewry—all this served to create a climate of emotional involvement building up to a pressure point almost too painful to bear.

## Days of Trial, Triumph, and Awe

Even before the fighting—which after its initial shock served as a release valve to the unbearable pressure—Jews were as one in their determination not to remain silent or inactive. The evasion of responsibility on the part of the Western Powers evoked among Jewry a unanimous outpouring of the will to *do*, a will that became the more passionate as the erosion of the U.N. became the more evident, a will that moved every Jew to offer of himself to the security of Israel. The duplicity of diplomacy served but to awaken a determination not to allow Jewish blood to become *hefker* again. . . .

Even during this early period of world paralysis and Arab aggression through the blockade of Akaba, Jews were beginning to experience the stirrings of teshuvah—in the sense of an awareness that Israel was alone—except for G-d—who had never declared His neutrality. The *T'hillim* became the constant companion of the shul Jew and the words of David became more meaningful, current, and significant with each passing day. The spirit of unity was on the upsurge as all Jews had but one concern—Israel—the land and its people. The phrase "as one man with one heart" became a reality—and Israel became—to all—a symbol of the indomitable Jewish spirit and its will to live.

The inevitable conflagration which followed the confrontation resulted in an amazing release of Jewish emotion, which though partially repressed had been as ready for explosion as the powder-keg of the Middle East itself.

None who lived through the Six Days, June 5-10, will ever forget the continuing hours of awesome fear, cautious optimism, exultant relief, pride, and joy—emotions which followed in electric succession. Many compared the victory of little Israel, against seemingly insurmountable odds, to that of David and Goliath. To the more sensitive, Torah-oriented Jew it was comparable rather to the story of Purim—for had we not witnessed the recurrence of *v'nehafoch hu*—all was turned about! Nasser, so proud and haughty one day, suddenly ground to the dust; the massed might of the Arab forces shattered; the indecision of the Western Powers countered by the bold, decisive action of the Israelis; the U.N. so reluctant to commit itself, suddenly galvanized into frantic action; the swiftness of Jewish triumph firing the imagination and admiration of men everywhere—elevating and ennobling their spirits. Vulnerable, tiny Israel *alone* and isolated was swiftly catapulted into a position of the strongest, most potent force in the Middle East. The similarity to Haman and Mordecai was so startling that one had to appreciate that here was a *ness nistar*, G-d manifesting His rule and will through the instrument of a revived, resolute, courageous and committed Israel!

This was not simply a military victory but a moral one. Practically speaking, it should never have happened, and thousands of words were written attempting to explain why it did happen. To the Jew, however, it was quite clear that G-d had not forsaken us and had once again demonstrated that the "guardian of Israel does not slumber or sleep." Even those who would not mar their analysis with the word "miracle" sensed that the world had witnessed a glorious chapter in the history of Israel when men were at their finest—rising to a moment of greatness.

Success, however, cannot properly be grasped in the measurable terms of how many tanks and airplanes destroyed, so much territory conquered, or the number of casualties and prisoners of war. The subtle aspect of success is what counts. What effect did these events have upon us—the Jewish people? We know of the repercussions which reverberated throughout the society of nations; the political upheavals, the revised military balance of power, the radical changes in the geography and demography of Israel and her neighbors—but what has all this meant to us—the Jewish people?

Let us attempt to place some of our reactions into proper perspective, based upon personal observation and the evaluation of intelligent and sensitive individuals.

First, the challenge and response, the trial and triumph of the Israelis evoked a profound sense of pride among all Jews. Understandably the degree and kind of pride varied with the values and sophistication of individual Jews, but every Jew felt a sense of *ga'avah*—of *shtoltz*, **of glorious pride**. The depth of our feeling was doubtless intensified because for the past many decades we had had so little cause for self-esteem. Who but a Jew had felt for so many years frustration and fear, the bitter taste of anguish and abject despair, the constant humiliating role of victim and vanquished? The glorious victory of the Israelis, with whom we so closely

## Days of Trial, Triumph, and Awe

identified ourselves, restored our self-respect, our sense of glory and grandeur which had so long been stripped from us and robbed from our children, as we were reduced to objects of ridicule and contempt.

To the Jew of the Siddur the words "who girdest Israel with might" became meaningful, and the phrase "who crownest Israel with glory" fraught with significance. He felt that his pleading question "Wherefore should the nations say, 'where now is their G-d?'" had been answered!

Further, the dramatic occurrences in Israel awakened within the hearts and souls of many the *pintele yid*—the dormant sense of belonging to and believing in the k'lal Yisroel and the G-d of Israel. There are rare moments that are so deeply moving, that they uncover this inner, concealed reservoir of faith in the heart of every Jew. The S'fath Emeth explains that the reason the month of Ellul has as its *mazol*—its Zodiac sign—a young maiden is to express the thought that in every Jew there is a part of his soul that is virginal—pure, untouched, unsullied by the mundane material world—and as one approaches, during Ellul, the Days of Awe this chaste, incorrupt "pintele" is uncovered and draws him back to his G-d and people. The crisis confronting Israel and the deliverance of our brethren from the forces that enveloped them had this same effect—it uncovered and awakened this inner pure "point" of Jewish identity and loyalty within many Jews who had removed themselves, or just drifted away from the mainstream of Judaism and had become estranged from the people of Israel.

Again, this experience welded together the Jewish people at a time when the need for unity was imperative. Many divisive forces and factors—religious and ideological—were at play for so many years that we had almost forgotten we were one people! The threat to Israel's existence served to remind us that we are "one people on this earth." In addition to the welcome spirit of unity there also was manifested a dazzling display of generosity which had rarely before, if ever, been demonstrated by any people. Jews who had never participated in matters of tzedokah involved themselves wholeheartedly and many who had established a modest level of giving elevated their sights and extended themselves in a manner which aroused the wonder and admiration of the non-Jewish world. The thousands of young volunteers from many countries who flocked to

## Days of Trial, Triumph, and Awe

Israel to help her in her hour of need demonstrated that the enthusiasm of idealism and desire for service was still very much alive in the hearts of our young people.

Finally, the impact made by the capture of the old city of Jerusalem, and to a lesser degree Bethlehem and Hebron, was so great that it defies description and will doubtless be impossible to really recapture in future years. Although the Western Wall (*Kothel Ma'arovi*) had always possessed a magnetism and mystique for Jews over the centuries, the inability to touch its stones for nineteen years had intensified its hold and holiness to us. The spiritual awakening accompanying the return to the Wall was an amazing revelation of how profound is the inherent, the invisible attachment of Jews to their heritage. The fervor, fever, and frantic exhilaration which the retaking of the old city of Jerusalem evoked among the Israelis and Jews throughout the world overshadowed even the startling accomplishments and achievements in Sinai, Syria, and Sharm El Sheikh. This was an unexpected prize, an unanticipated gift, the realization of a dream, the fulfillment of prophetic promise—and to many the advent of the Messianic era. The stirrings of teshuvah took on more substance and sincerity—for who could fail to recognize here the answer to the age-old prayer "and to Jerusalem Thy city, in mercy return"—an answer which brought a positive response by many who had been estranged for so long, and yet hastened to make a pilgrimage to this holiest of places and pay homage to the place from whence the *Shechinah*, the Divine Presence, had never departed.

"To be privileged once again to visit the Tomb of Rachel, and the Cave of Machpelah—what a *zechus* to be granted all this—and how we must learn to appreciate this great 'merit'—which has been given to our generation!"—this is the sentiment expressed by so many. A heartening, inspiring aspect is that so many young people both in Israel and here feel so strongly about the holy places now in our hands—accessible once again to k'lal Yisroel—relics awaiting the return of their children!

The fervor of the Jews is of course equaled by the furor of the nations. Jerusalem has ever-fired the imagination and passions of man. The bitter fighting followed by angry debate is further

## Days of Trial, Triumph, and Awe

enflamed by Israeli unification of Old with New Jerusalem. We are not concerned here with the political wisdom or diplomatic good judgment of Israel's statesmen. We do submit, however, that only those who sat on the ground Tisha B'av for so many years; who recited the prayers of "O rebuild Jerusalem the Holy City," "And may our eyes be granted to witness thy return to Zion" and "To Jerusalem, thy city, in mercy return" for so many centuries, can truly understand what Jerusalem means to Jews. To misread this fervent attachment or misunderstand its implications would be a tragic miscalculation on the part of the nations.

The political situation is still in a state of flux and the diplomatic battles rage unabated. What the future holds in store regarding borders, peace treaties, and Israel's relationship to the family of nations is obscure and disquieting. Perhaps we Jews have suffered too much to allow ourselves the luxury of fully enjoying our moment of sweet victory. Be that as it may, we are apprehensive as we await to see whether we can win the peace as decisively as the war.

\* \* \*

This much however is clear: The glorious events of the first weeks of Sivan 5727 moved, awakened, and aroused us as a people, in a manner rarely experienced by any people. It may well be the magical key that opens the box which contains the keys to other problems of Israel—the land and the people. Just as military and political analysts recognize that Israel and her position in the Middle East can never be the same again, that the past is obsolete, so must we realize that our relationship to Eretz Yisroel and to the k'lal Yisroel can never be the same. However, in our case, the historic past is not obsolete, for we were strangely and wonderfully thrust back into the past as we were catapulted into the challenging future. Holmes once said: "Man's mind stretched to a new idea never goes back to its original dimensions." All that transpired has stretched not only the borders but our minds as well, hopefully never to return to the narrow dimensions of the past.

The Divine plan begins to emerge. How vividly and dramatically have we of this era been reminded that only by drawing our inspiration from the Wall, the Tomb, and the Cave can we find the strength and vision to build for the future.

## Chapter 17

# Israel's State of Mind — Israel's State of War

*A Post Six-Day War Analysis**

The conclusion is inescapable. The State of Israel, while not a state *at war*, is in a state of war. Her borders are expanded and new, but so are the conditions along these borders. In the North, East and along the Suez, artillery duels, air dog fights, and commando raids, are so commonplace that it takes something really unusual to capture the headlines. Two years have passed since the Six-Day War, but—as a recent cartoon has one Israeli soldier saying plaintively to another as they sit in their foxhole—"The Six-Day War is now over 700 days old." The Four Power talks have apparently failed; the Jarring mission is quiescent and the portents for peace are painfully dim.

But, it is not our purpose to write a political or military analysis of the Arab-Israel dilemma; what concerns us here is the effect all this is having upon the Israeli national character—and above all the *Jewish* character of the Jews living in Israel, under these tragic and tense conditions. A state of war—be it small and limited, or large and full-scale—must create a climate and atmosphere charged with attitudes, and permeated with perspectives that are far different than those which prevail in an environment of peace and tranquility. The Vietnam war, thousands of miles away, affected the political and social climate of a country of 200 million—where depersonalization is the norm; how much more so the effect of a continuous battle hitting so close to home, where everyone seems to know each soldier who falls at the front?

---
*This chapter was written two years after the Six-Day War. It is still very relevant.

## Israel's State of Mind — Israel's State of War

A state of war has ever left its indelible imprint upon people as individuals and as a nation. The value of human life, economic and social priorities, the cultural and spiritual quality of a society at war—these are a few vital areas which are perforce colored and shaped by constant violence, terrorism, destruction and danger. How have our people fared since the summer of '67? And while we are examining the state of our people in Israel we would also ask, what has the world remembered and what have they forgotten in the brief period of two years?

The Torah is most concerned about the method of waging war and its effect upon the soldier. War is not inevitable, but it is also not always avoidable. The Torah laws regulating warfare—the unique exemptions from service, the recognition of man's moral vulnerability, the protection of natural resources, to mention but a few—are unique in the history of mankind. What we would stress, however, is the emphasis upon the holiness of the Jewish camp and the sacred value ascribed to each human life. The *parshah* of *Eglah Arufah* is interposed between two portions dealing with warfare to underscore this point. The Torah teaches that the life of a stranger—friendless, unknown and homeless—found murdered, presents a challenge of great importance and inherent spiritual value. The elders of Israel are held responsible for the victim, and even the Sanhedrin must send its emissaries to determine who shall bring the heifer and seek atonement. The wholesale shedding of blood in battle must not make us insensitive to the precious value of one Jewish soul. In this respect Israel today measures up admirably to the Torah standard. War casualties, reported as numbers and statistics in *The New York Times* are a profound personal loss in Israel. The loss of every soldier is felt most deeply: he is everyone's son, brother, husband. And this is not artificially stimulated to create heroes, to fan the flames of hatred for the enemy, or to keep military morale high. Anyone who has recently spent some time in Israel can attest to the sincerity and honesty of these heartfelt emotions. In this sense then the incessant warfare and daily casualties have not succeeded in cheapening human life. On the contrary it has made the Israeli deeply treasure, prize and appreciate every *yochid*.

A nation under arms, as Israel is, where the bulk of able-bodied men comprise a people's army, is prone to become a Prussian-like people: martial and warlike in temperament and disposition. A military posture may not become Jews, but it could well become a way of life, by necessity, and thereby also transform the mien and face of the new Israel. Thoughtful Israelis, including many of the secular camp, have feared this consequence of three wars in two decades and the continuing period of crisis and challenge which imposes upon the nation the need for increased military service. For a people steeped in the tradition and teaching of *Shalom* this is an ugly and unwanted image. Fighting, killing, planning military strategy and techniques, are alien to the Jewish spirit: they are engaged in with reluctance and distaste.

From all indications and reports, Israelis have not been transformed into a military people. Shortly after the Six-Day War a number of young kibbutz members who had participated in the fighting met to discuss their reactions. The tapes were edited and published in a volume called—*Siach Lochamim*—"Soldiers Talk." Mirrored in these most interesting comments are the doubts and determination of these young men, their qualms and convictions. Above all, in spite of their secularist point-of-view, there shines through a most revealing and heart-warming sense of compassion and control, of sensitivity and sincerity, and an abhorrence of bloodshed which one could never find among soldiers in other lands. A citizen soldier is still a farmer, professional, teacher, or workman, and the job of soldiering is only temporary, to be set aside as quickly as possible. The Israeli society is gripped by a military mood, but they have succeeded in refraining from becoming a militaristic people.

The primary victims of a nation at war are its national priorities. This was the problem of the United States, during the Vietnam War years. Housing, education, welfare, hunger and poverty are no longer the prime concern of a government that must produce munitions, arm and supply an army, and bend its best efforts toward the worst of all human endeavors—war. In Israel, although much sacrifice is demanded from the people in the form of taxes and general economic belt-tightening, nonetheless the needs of *olim*, of housing and welfare, are not shunted aside and lost in the frenzied attention paid to security. Education, its expansion and development, is very much at the top of the state's agenda. In the realm of

Torah study, never have so many yeshivoth and kollelim been developed and expanded as rapidly as they are in an Israel beleaguered by its enemies. Cultural activities flourish, the arts are respected, and here, as in the area of human values and the moral character of the nation, Israel has not permitted its sense of values and priorities to be distorted by the state of war.

On this level of *nissayon*, on this plateau of testing, Israel has passed the test—for the present. The descendants of the *Avos* have retained their compassion and concern for *man*—not to be confused with the specious, artificial concern for "mankind." The people, who descend from the *Am Ha'Torah* have not lost their collective character and the *Am Ha'sefer* still clings to the values and priorities befitting Jews.

There is another level of *nissayon*, however, where I fear Israel has not fared as well. Indeed in this area our fondest hopes may have been misplaced and, alas, our most cherished dreams shattered. I refer to the area of *emunah*—belief in the providence of the Almighty, the faith in G-d's special, unique, protection of *Am Yisroel* in *Eretz-Yisroel*. The faith in the *hashgochah* of the Almighty "whose eyes are upon this land from the beginning of the year to the end of each year." This special Providence, which was so apparent and open during the Six-Day War that even "non-believers" saw the miracles, has been denigrated, dismissed and denied. The reversion to a "my-strength-and-the-might-of-my-hand" philosophy is projected by far too many Israeli leaders.

Recently, in a televised interview with the Prime Minister and the Minister of Defense, the interviewer, a non-Jew, asked them if they felt that miracles akin to those related in the Bible had occurred in '67. He asked if they believed that G-d had intervened on the side of Israel as in days of old. *They both begged the question.* Mr. Dayan protested that he was not "orthodox"—hence apparently disqualifying himself from answering such a "religious" question. Mrs. Meir fielded the question with more finesse, but—with an audience numbering in the millions waiting for an answer to a most serious question—never rose to the challenge as a *Jewish* spokesman to proclaim a basic faith in the G-d of Israel. As diplomats the two no doubt had to choose their responses prudently and with caution, but had they acknowledged the intervention of *Ha'Shem* on the side of the Jews, the worst that could have happened would be that the Security Council might choose to censure the Almighty, and such displeasure expressed by the United Nations has never served as a deterrent to a brave and defiant Israel! We hasten to add, *l'kaf zechus*, that not all Israeli leaders are so reluctant to acknowledge our dependence upon the Almighty. The Speaker of the Knesset, Kadish Luz, though a non-observant veteran of the leftist Kibbutz Deganiah, in his address to the Israeli parliament on *Yom Ha'atzmaut* invoked the help of the Almighty and quoted the posuk: "... And as Moshe raised his hands Israel prevailed" with the classic interpretation of *Chazal*—as did President Shazar in his message. Unfortunately, the Israeli press, in most instances, saw fit to delete these pious wishes and prayers. To the world at large the image of Israel is rapidly and tragically becoming one of a pugnacious, audacious, arrogant people, albeit brave, courageous and heroic. The softening of this image, by simply being what we really are, a *Goy Kodosh*, or at least by recalling and revitalizing our status as the *Am Ha'Shem* would be helpful even diplomatically—but this seems to be too much to expect from non-believers who are committed to the Land and the People, to its history and folklore, but not to the fundamental of all *ikrim: Emunah ba'Shem*.

To the *ma'amin* this is extremely distressing and depressing. For our understanding of the Jewish army and its relationship to the G-d of Israel is special and unique. To us the events of two years ago, and subsequent developments, are seen as a call from on High. Not alone what is happening in Israel but throughout the world cries out to mankind in general and Yisroel in particular to make a *Cheshbon Hanefesh* in this epoch—when we hear "the footsteps of Moshiach." Of course, to properly understand and evaluate the events in which one plays a role—especially an important and decisive one—demands a breadth of vision and a depth of understanding, which in turn requires a deep faith and a rejection of one's personal involvement and concern. This, tragically, most of Israel's top political and military leaders lack.

It is interesting that the pioneering spirit of Israel was called *chalutziut* and the original settlers *chalutzim*. What is the origin of this word? We find it twice in rapid succession in one *parshah* of the Torah (*Matos*), *hechaltzu me'itchem anashim l'tzava*—Moshe

## Israel's State of Mind — Israel's State of War

commands the Jews to *arm* themselves for the battle against Midian. Again when he speaks to the tribes of Gad and Reuven he says "if you will *arm (techaltzu)* yourselves to go before *Ha'Shem* to war." Gad and Reuven also use the same expression—"we ourselves (*ne'chaletz*) will be ready armed to go before the children of Israel." Yet we also find this word in connection with *chalitzah*: to loosen or remove the shoe of the brother who refuses to wed the childless widow of his deceased brother. Obviously the root of the word *chalotz* means not simply "to arm" but to *remove*. The *S'fas Emes* therefore interprets the phrase in *Matos* to mean: *"Remove from yourselves"*—divest yourselves from your own desires and ambitions, and only then can you be a Jewish soldier! Even after the tribes of Gad and Reuven pledge themselves to be chalutzim, Moshe is dissatisfied, for they have not mentioned the key words "before G-d," hence they have not divested themselves of their own pride and vanity; how then can they be true *chalutzim*? What we desperately need in Israel today—in military and government circles—is *chalutziot* as envisioned by Torah.

As these words are written, the political portents for Israel are ominous. France re-affirms its embargo on arms and planes to Israel. U Thant seems determined to re-enact his role as fomentor of war in the Middle East. The United Nations is silent regarding Egyptian aggressive acts and is vociferous in chastising and scolding Israel for its position and policy in Jerusalem—with the United States concurring. The World Council of Churches and the Vatican are busy reiterating their anti-Israel stand on the Holy City. The world has so soon forgotten the events of '67. *But have we also not forgotten?* The nations of the world have ever re-acted to our posture and position. When Israel forgets the miracles and providence of the Almighty the *Umos Ha'olom* lose their fear and reverence and act according to their natural instincts—which is invariably antagonistic to *Am Yisroel*.

The prophet Jeremiah laments—"Neither said they, Where is *Ha'Shem* that brought us up from Egypt, that led us through the wilderness." Mendel Hirsch, son of Samson Raphael Hirsch, makes the following observation. In moments of travail and trial they did not ask—what is the will of G-d, what does *Ha'Shem* have to say to us—what is His will? And he goes on to note that the present tense

## Israel's State of Mind — Israel's State of War

is used by the prophet when he speaks of the exodus and journey in the desert: "Who *brings* us, (constantly) out of Egypt"—"Who leads us (ever) through the wilderness." Certainly we must not allow ourselves to forget the *Chasdei Ha'Shem*—who revealed His concern and brought salvation two short years ago, and fail to ask *"Ayeh Ha'Shem?"* in all of our diplomatic and military endeavors. This is the area of Israel's vulnerability. The test is great and the *nissayon* most difficult: to withstand the temptation of absorbing and emulating modern man's malady of taking undue pride in one's own strength and prowess.

And so as we study Israel's people, and their condition as a self-respecting proud people on their own land, we are confronted with this duality as we observe the two areas where they are being tested and tried by history and *hashgocha*. We are filled with pride and joy at the basic majesty of people who have withstood not only their enemies on the field of battle, but the greater, more serious threat of inner erosion and destruction of national character. We are dismayed and fearful as we witness a reliance upon personal skill and might, competence and courage—which may be heroic in the eyes of those who measure by the yardstick of secular, material values—but is tragic and ultimately dangerous to those who believe profoundly that our *gevurah* and *netzach* depends upon the *gevurah* of He who is *Netzach*.

An oriental philosopher once said "The meaning of a room is not in the four walls but in the space between them." The same is true of a country's boundariesT what is in the space between them is all important—its people, their values, their collective character, their cherished goals as well as their noble past. *Am Yisroel* in *Eretz Yisroel* has a historic responsibility, as does k'lal Yisroel everywhere, during these days of trial when the "voice of the dove is heard in the land," as the Vilner Gaon refers to the advent of Moshiach in his sefer *Kol Hator*. We must recognize the awesome burden that has been placed upon this generation. To fail is a failure to hear the call of destiny. To meet this challenge successfully will be a *zechus* and triumph that will alter the course of all *Mankind*.

Chapter 18

# A Response to the Yom Kippur War, in Retrospect

Momentous events tend to evoke reactions, but in truth, responses are demanded. More than a mere emotional reaction to a stimulus, a response constitutes a reply, an attempt to answer questions one cannot avoid.

When the Yom Kippur War erupted, Jews throughout the world understandably recoiled with horror and followed up with a sacrificial outpouring of support for, and solidarity with, the beleaguered Jewish state. Only when the battle-scarred weeks passed were profound emotions replaced with questions — How did it happen? Why were we so unprepared? . . . And the reassessment began.

Bit by bit, the myths had evaporated: the invincibility of the Israeli defense forces . . . the inability of the Arabs to use modern weaponry and their lack of will to fight . . . the Western world's sympathy and support for Israel. New facts entered the scene: the Arab oil weapon . . . Israel's shaky economy . . . the ongoing mobilization of civilians . . . her demoralization by internal political bickering.

Now that a few years have passed since that eventful October, it is vital to view the events in a Torah perspective. How should we respond to this abrupt, radical transformation of the stability of the Jewish State and the dark future that seems to threaten? The purpose of this chapter is to sift through the reactions, to find some responses that have been recorded, and to suggest others that as yet may not have been formulated.

The early years of the state, with its attendant growth and exciting newness, projected a picture-postcard view of Israel. After so long a period of dispersion and national non-identity in the conventional

## A Response to the Yom Kippur War, in Retrospect

sense, Israel was recognized as a nation among nations with all the trappings of a modern state — U.N. membership, ambassadors, ministers, an army and air force. The sense of exhilaration experienced during that first decade of statehood was only briefly interrupted by the 1956 War. The 1967 Six-Day War, however, electrified the world and elevated the spirit of Jews everywhere; its impact upon Soviet Jewry was truly miraculous. And the sense of euphoria lasted — until the bubble was pricked in October, '73.

The twenty-five years of Israel's independence with all its accomplishments and sense of national pride had convinced the overwhelming majority of Israelis that the philosophy of political Zionism had been justified: once Jews had a state of their own, the result would be "normalization of the Jewish people." A generation of Israelis had been reared with this idea that Israel was like unto other nations, no longer the isolated, dispersed, wandering people.

Normalcy, once realized, exploded with the Yom Kippur War. A leading Israeli novelist and journalist, Hanoch Bartov, expressed this in a *Commentary* article (March '74): "In the glowing aftermath of the Six Day War we lost all sense of reality, all sense of what it still means to be Jewish in a hostile world." The title of his article says it all — "Back to Abnormal." To a young Israeli, normalcy means being a nation among nations no different than others. When this illusion was shattered, it meant that we were still abnormal.

This, however, is a fallacious interpretation of the Jewish condition. To the Torah Jew, normalcy has always meant being totally different. Following the Six-Day War, Dr. Yaakov Herzog delivered a most perceptive paper, "Behold A Nation That Dwells Alone." He cautioned his fellow Israelis to disabuse themselves of modern political Zionist ideology, for since the beginning of our history as a people, "aloneness" has been our normal condition. It is precisely our isolation from the family of nations and our unique position of a distinct entity in a hostile world that grants us our identity. Bilam understood this well when he said "Behold a people that dwells alone, not reckoned among nations" (Bamidbar 23,9). Contrast the point of view of a traditionalist with that of a secularist. Using Herzog's historic approach, Bartov's article would have been entitled "Back to Normal"!

One post-Yom Kippur response, then: Not only are we destined to be an "*Am l'vadad* — a nation alone," but more profoundly, our true strength lies precisely in our aloneness. Not only those reared in a Torah atmosphere but even secular Jews are reconsidering as they contemplate the bitter fruits of the past fifteen months. Perhaps they will yet fathom the wisdom in the Netziv's interpretation of *"Hain am l'vadad yishkon bagoyim lo yischashov* — Behold a Nation that dwells alone, not reckoned among the nations": If they are content to be *"levadad* — alone," then *"yishkon* — they will dwell in tranquility." If, however, *"bagoyim"* — they insist upon being a nation among nations, then *"lo yis'chashov"* — they will be totally without importance in the eyes of the world, and vulnerable as well.

Witnessing destruction and death, experiencing the aloofness of an insensitive world community surrendering to oil blackmail, many Jews returned to their own source and to their own roots — if only for a moment. The sober spiritual revival at the time of the Yom Kippur War, the demand for *tefillin* by Israeli soldiers, manifested an overwhelming desire to identify with the authentic spirit of Israel and to reach out to the G-d of Israel who neither slumbers nor sleeps. The significance of the war breaking out on Yom Kippur could not be ignored, and somehow every Jew was shaken to his soul.

In this climate of introspection, sensitive Jews all over the world were in a mood for reappraisal and even ripe for persuasion. Unfortunately, world Jewry's huge communal machinery was geared exclusively to fund-raising, not to soul-searching; while the Torah world's voice was relatively mute. As a parallel, with different results, one might take note of how Mordechai in ancient Persia did not attempt to raise funds to counter Haman's price of ten thousand silver pieces which he had paid to obtain license from the king to destroy the Jews. Mordechai understood this horrible decree as a signal from Heaven that the Jews deserved punishment for their transgressions. Mordechai was determined not to divert the Jews from a response of repentance and a radical change of life-style and values — their only salvation — by making an appeal for funds.

In a time of emergency, there is a tendency to find the lowest common denominator as a basis for unity rather than challenging people to excellence, which can also hold a nation together. Unfortunately, the broad community did not have such leadership in October '73, and although the funds raised for U.J.A. and Bonds were necessary, we must ask if that was the *total* response expected of

## A Response to the Yom Kippur War, in Retrospect

world Jewry when a divine signal was beamed to us. Every *ma'amin*, once the initial shock wore off, certainly read that signal to mean that after twenty-five years of statehood and four bloody wars, we could not rely on our own might or on the mercy of the world; we desperately are in need of G-d's protection, which is only granted if we are worthy.

The experience of the last two wars can be seen as part of a series of lessons in faith. The Six-Day War can be interpreted as a call to a recognition of divine protection peculiar to *Eretz Yisroel* — a call transmitted through fantastic, swift victories. On *Yom Kippur* and *Succos* 5734, this call was transmitted through a miracle of a different kind, revealed through pain and suffering, temporary setbacks, and subsequent triumph. For there were many miracles which became apparent with the passage of time: the Egyptian and Syrian armies' decision not to penetrate more deeply into thinly defended Israel; Sadat's refusal to agree to a cease fire when the Egyptians were in a most favorable, forward position; the Israelis' successful counter-offensive on both fronts; the audacious crossing of the canal, cutting off the Egyptian Third Army — all as miraculous as many of the feats recorded during the Six-Day War. The military observer and political analyst marvels . . . but the believer sees in all this the *hashgochas Hashem*.

Rabbi Eliyahu Eliezer Dessler speaks of two kinds of miracles in *Michtav M'Eliyahu*. Both are meant to impress man that what he witnesses is not a natural occurrence, but G-d's revelation. At times, miracles are wrought for Israel's obvious benefit and welfare; other times, miracles occur in a "sea of suffering," when G-d seemingly assists our enemies. Then, the purpose is to bring Israel back to G-d. When they do repent, the nature of the miracle changes suddenly and dramatically from the negative, destructive kind to the positive, saving one. . . . When we review the eventful days of that Fall, we can see these words translated into reality. However, as mentioned, we somehow failed to bring these truths to our people, whose hearts were open at that time.

Although the teshuva thoughts of so many Israelis proved to be transitory, the Yom Kippur trauma left a deep imprint on many of their attitudes. A number of years ago, the publisher of a new magazine declared his ambition to "start little insurrections in the realm of people's convictions." The Yom Kippur War, its early frightening days and the huge toll it exacted, has brought forth a veritable revolution in the cherished convictions of many Israelis. Beyond realizing their terrible isolation in the world community, their self-confidence also suffered a severe blow, and trust in their military leadership was shattered. At the same time, the universal Jewish response this War aroused also gave them a renewed appreciation of the oneness of k'lal Yisroel — a salvation with no individual, towering saviors.

The Israeli election results demonstrated a similar anomaly — anger at the establishment, yet distrust of untried others. This much is certain, there are no heroes in Israel today. True, the eclipse of heroes is a common phenomenon today — be it in the United States, or throughout the Western world. But the transitory nature of men's prestige and fame was most dramatically demonstrated in Israel when the Agranat Report was issued. Who would have believed, a few years ago, that Golda Meir and Moshe Dayan would be scathingly criticized by a committee of inquiry and become the targets of angry demonstrators? That glory passes and the armor of heroes becomes tarnished is not unknown to sensible, mature men, but in this case, the fall came with deadly swiftness.

Rather than lament the toppling of heroes, this can be seen as an advantage, a reminder of the traditional Jewish attitude toward temporal heroes. Long before the non-hero became the protagonist of modern literature, Jewish tradition rejected the larger-than-life figure. In the Haggadah of Pesach, Moshe is not even mentioned so as to focus exclusively on the Almighty's deeds and not on those of any man who is but the instrument of divine will. The collective dedication of the Jewish people, bolstered by faith and courage, is more important than individual stars.

We have shown that a number of reassessments resulted from this war: a new understanding of Jewish normalcy, a degree of *teshuva*, a search for roots of strength and dignity, a recognition of Jewish solidarity and of the world's indifference to our fate, as well as the toppling of long-standing heroes. But coupled with these lessons we detect a most disquieting outgrowth of the Yom Kippur War. For the first time since the state was established, there is a subtle sense of

## A Response to the Yom Kippur War, in Retrospect

yiush — if not surrender or despair, then dejection, weariness, and apprehension. The high casualty rate of a war which really accomplished naught, and actually placed an Egyptian presence on the eastern bank of the Suez and Syrians in Kuneitra, is a deep scar on the collective soul of Israel. Murderous terrorist attacks have left the populace shaken and deeply vulnerable. Add to this the fear and anxiety of future political developments, constant pressures for more concessions from Israel, and we can appreciate how nationalism and the patriotism of the average citizen are being put to the test. — Not all are passing this difficult *nissayon*.

There are those who falter — for their god of "my might and the strength of my arm" has failed them. There are, however, many who are firm and resolute, the majority of whom are possessed by a love and loyalty to *Eretz Yisroel* that transcends nationalism and patriotism. Without thought of abandoning the state, these men and women have an attachment to the Holy Land formed by the special dimension of *kedushas Ha'aretz* — the sanctity of the land and the historic destiny of the people of Israel tied to this land as part of its covenant with the Almighty. Their determination is unaffected by the events of the past few years. I believe even secular Zionists who are knowledgeable and fair would agree, although reluctantly, that the chances of *shomrei Torah* Jews becoming *yordim* are far less than that of secular-educated *sabras*. By the same token, the reservoir of potential *olim* from the free world is far greater from this religious element — more so than from the non-religious Jews who may be enthusiastic in their support of Israel but whose personal commitment to the land is superficial. How ironic, and yet so logical from a Jewish historic perspective, that after a quarter century of statehood the hope for Zion lies more with those elements who have been labeled as "non-" or even "anti-" Zionist rather than with card-carrying Zionists! Another myth exploded by the Yom Kippur war.

Consider a *New York Times* interview last summer with five Israeli high school seniors. The correspondent spoke to a cross-section of Israeli students representing an ethnic and political mix — *sabra* and immigrant, Ashkenazi and Sephardi, liberal and right-wing — but, unfortunately, all secularly oriented. They revealed a most disturbing picture of Israeli youth, expressing so many doubts and questions about our historic right to Israel. Shallow commitment and very little Jewish passion and devotion can be found in their remarks. A primary concern seemed to be for the poor Palestinians whose rights they had suddenly discovered! What is missing is far more important and revealing than what is present in this interview:

One of the young people lamented the loss of the pioneering spirit of the parent generation. Another used suffering under Nazi persecution as justification for the Jewish claim to the land. Not one, however, spoke of the special purpose of our peoplehood and our covenantal right to *Eretz Yisroel*. Had there been present but one of the tens of thousands of observant young Jews and Jewesses who live in Israel today, the readers of the *New York Times* would be aware of their profound commitment to the land based upon the unique unalterable relationship of Israel to G-d. They would have been introduced to a segment of the population whose idealism and devotion is not less than that of the parents of these hesitant youngsters who nostalgically envy the *"chalutziot"* spirit — a spirit that can never be transmitted from father to son as effectively as the Torah spirit. Those whose attitude to Israel is shaped by factors far more sacred and far more profound than nationalism and patriotism are the maximalists in loyalty and perseverance, whom no wars or political pressures can move from their determination.

We have mentioned the religious revival that surfaced during each of Israel's wars. The return is always a temporary one, due to the secular "non-Jewish" environment prevailing in Israel. While it is unreasonable to simply hope for a lasting transformation, it is proper to examine, in the light of all that has been mentioned above, another question not sufficiently considered in recent years: The average Israeli citizen must be impressed by the consistent warmth and devotion displayed by observant Jews both in Israel and throughout the world in every critical period confronting Israel. If Israelis have learned that their only reliable friends are other Jews, they should also have learned that within k'lal Yisroel, the observant, Torah-Jew is the most trustworthy of all. In spite of constant violations of religious sensibilities over the years, and in spite of frequent tensions between Torah Jewry and the state, the loyalty and profound commitment of observant Jews to the *yishuv* has at no time wavered. Government leaders know this full well, and perhaps this may have allowed the government to withhold from the Torah community concessions similar to those made to the deviationist camp. In a crunch, they could always depend on their support anyway.

In contrast to this truth, the public relations machinery of major Jewish organizations, including that of the Zionist groups, has succeeded in creating a climate of distrust by placing unfair labels of *"Sonei Yisroel"* on certain circles of the Torah community because of their religious demands. At the very same time, they give polite ear to unconscionable threats of those who are more acceptable to them — spokesmen for the Reform and Conservative movements who during the "Who Is A Jew" controversy actually threatened to cut off financial support for the government if the legitimacy of their movements was not officially recognized — the type of threat the orthodox community never dared make. The question must therefore be asked: Why have Torah Jews been unable to project their true image?

Indeed part of our response to the Yom Kippur War, must be to question ourselves: why have we failed to impress our Israeli brethren with our sense of brotherhood with them — that we are the most trustworthy, concerned friends they possess? Could it be that, after twenty-five years of statehood, a major challenge facing orthodox Jewry, regardless of party affiliation, is to change somehow our image from intransigents to inspirers, from religious authoritarians who want to impose their restrictive way of life upon a resisting populace, to custodians of our people's ideals and historic faith? We have learned that we cannot *capture* the imaginations of our Israeli brothers; but perhaps we can still *captivate* them. In today's climate of doubt and despair, which seems to have enveloped so many Israelis, we may be able to reach many of them by bringing them *chizuk* — a spiritual reinforcement that can best be conveyed by men and women, especially young people, who are themselves imbued with faith and trust, and can transmit this spirit with sincerity.

Would Israelis not be receptive to this kind of approach, stripped of political ambitions and goals, geared only to demonstrate that all

## A Response to the Yom Kippur War, in Retrospect

Jews are brothers, and that the new gods have failed them as those that failed our forefathers in this Holy Land in the time of the Judges and the Kings? Perhaps this will help formulate our *teshuva*, our response to the traumatic experiences of the Yom Kippur War, Kiryat Sh'moneh, and Maalot. Ha'shem must be asking something of *Bnei Torah*, as well as kibbutzniks, of *frum* Jews as well as the cafe patrons on Dizengoff, of *ma'aminim* as well as *kofrim*. If they were guilty of relying too much on "my might and the strength of my hand," then we may be guilty of an excessive "peace unto my soul" syndrome.

To argue, as many of us have in past years, that we need not defend our love of Israel and all its inhabitants, is not the point. To protest with righteous indignation that our credentials of *Ahavas Eretz Yisroel* are far superior to those who question them, is not the issue. What is important to understand is that communicating this in the arena of public opinion can be almost as important as the unrecognized fact, that appearance is a vital necessity in the battle of ideas and in our ability to influence others. Toward this end, it seems to me, we must bend our every effort.

There is frequently a lot of posturing and pretense in the meaningless actions and pronouncements of Jewish organizations. It has well been said, however, that pretense often hides, not evil, but emptiness. It is time for us to fill the void of secular Zionism with an imaginative program of substance, which can only be done through the power of Torah truth and integrity, in a spirit of *Ahavas-Yisroel* and-*Eretz Yisroel*. The way has been shown by a number of commendable projects — some sponsored by political parties, others totally outside of partisan activity. It is only with substantive sincerity that we can hope to evoke a more lasting response from our brethren rather than the frenetic short-lived outbursts of Jewish identity, fired only by emergencies.'

The times are changing. Many individuals are beginning to question their cherished values and scale of priority. In 1967 car bumper stickers proclaimed "All honor to the Israeli army." Today they read "Israel, trust in the Al-mighty." Should we not consider some little insurrections in our own position as well, and heed the signals from on high that call to us for a greater measure of unity and a greater effort to bring the Torah concept of *Eretz Yisroel* to Jews everywhere?

## Chapter 19

# Zionism, Judaism, and Eretz Yisroel

Terms and phrases which we use constantly become overly familiar and tend to blunt our analytical powers. We have a tendency to repeat phrases and labels without really considering their true meaning. Knee-jerk reaction and reflex response to certain names are, therefore, quite common, but when we are confronted by changing circumstances and challenged by antagonists to define them, we are hard put to do so intelligently.

Since the turn of the century the term 'Zionism' has become a common household word in Jewish circles and with the establishment of the State of Israel, it became known to the world at large. To the average Jew, it conjured up an image of his ancient homeland and the political movement founded by Theodor Herzl. Not until last year (1975), when the "Zionism is Racism" resolution was passed by the United Nations General Assembly, did many individuals appreciate the need to carefully and intelligently define just what is meant by the word "Zionism."

In the emotional aftermath of this obscene resolution, many responded by asserting that Zionism is the equivalent of Judaism, while others claimed that Zionism was the Jewish National Liberation movement. Both of these extravagant reactions were incorrect and it is, therefore, important to define Zionism from a historic traditional perspective, assigning it to a proper, balanced position within the body of Jewish thought.

The word Zion appears in the Bible countless times and is familiar to anyone who uses the Siddur. While etymologically it means a sign or symbol, the term refers primarily to a place, namely the mountain in Jerusalem. The name evolved into one by which Jerusalem, the land of Israel, and even the nation, was known and thereby became

## Zionism, Judaism, and Eretz Yisroel

symbolic of Jewish nationhood and statehood. "For from Zion shall come forth the law and the word of G-d from Jerusalem" is among the more familiar quotations indicating that Zion also represents the source of Torah and since the Sanhedrin had its headquarters on the Temple mount, all decisions of Jewish law emanated from Zion as well. When the prophet exclaims "for Zion's sake I will not be silent" he sets the eternal emotional tone which strikes a responsive chord in the heart of Jews, reflecting their constant profound concern for the security of the Jewish people in the land of Israel. The expression in our daily prayers "May our eyes be privileged to witness your return to Zion" indicates the eternal longing of Jews everywhere, and at all times, for their redemption and return to the Holy Land. When one sits shivah, *chas v'shalom*, he is consoled by the comforter with the phrase "May you be comforted among the mourners of Zion and Jerusalem," which demonstrates the inexorable intimate link of the individual Jew with his homeland. From these quotations we see that Zion is synonymous with the land of Israel and the people of Israel. Our Sages, however, have told us that only in one biblical sentence is the *nation* of Israel referred to as Zion: "And I have put my words in thy mouth, and have covered thee in the shadow of my hand that I may plant the heavens and lay the foundations of the earth, and say unto Zion; thou art my people" (Isaiah 51).

The term 'Zionism,' coined by Nathan Birnbaum, came to the fore at the end of the nineteenth century with the awakening of Jewish longing to return to the land and the founding of various movements to translate this dream into a reality. Doubtless, the name became popularized with the convening of the first Zionist congress in 1898. With the passage of time the term 'Zionism' became synonomous with this political movement. After the establishment of the state in 1948, 'Zionism' was used by anti-Israel elements as a convenient code word, which shielded them from the onerous label of anti-Semitism, whenever they attacked the State of Israel and the Jewish nation. This, of course, reached its crescendo and climax with the 'Zionism is Racism' resolution.

To properly understand the role of the land of Israel in Jewish thought one must go back to our origins which, in turn, requires study of our roots as recorded in the Torah. The creation of the Jewish people, as pointed out by Samson R. Hirsch, was similar to

## Zionism, Judaism, and Eretz Yisroel

that of the creation of the world, i.e., *ex nihilo*, "something from nothing." Unlike other nations, the Jewish people did not evolve but were called into being. The bondage in Egypt is referred to as an "iron furnace" in which Israel's being and character were forged. Their exodus from the land of bondage was not merely a process of national liberation and freedom, but had a purpose and goal, to become a "Kingdom of priests and a holy nation." The land of Israel, destined to be their eventual homeland, was promised many years before to the patriarchs as part of a covenant with the Almighty. The early period of wandering in the desert was meant to serve as one of training and education; but they became a people and nation even before they entered the land, once they accepted the Torah. "This day thou art become a people" is said by Moses to Israel when they enter the covenant with the Almighty. It is the Torah and their covenant with the Almighty that forms and shapes them into a nation. It is not uncommon for nations to have a government in exile *after* they have been driven from their land. Ours is the only case in history where we were a nation even before we had a land, a state, or national government!

Nonetheless, the full fruition and total development of Israel as a nation could not be realized until they had established themselves in the promised land of Eretz Yisroel. The land of Israel is the vehicle of national fulfillment and only in their own land can Jews realize their full potential as a "light to the nations." However, important as the land was and is, the existence of Israel as a people was not dependent upon it, even after being driven from the land, just as it was not dependent upon it before we came into the land. As mentioned above, when the prophet refers to the people of Israel as "Zion" he does so in conjunction with our commitment to G-d and his Torah which plants heaven (i.e., spiritual values) within every Jew, and has the ability of establishing even the 'land' within every Jew, no matter where he may reside! Jeremiah, the prophet of destruction and dispersal, also conveys this thought when he states "the sanctuary of the Almighty are they" indicating that even the destruction of the Temple did not sever Israel's relationship with the Almighty or abrogate their covenant with Him. The *Shechinah* still remains within every Jewish household and Kehillah. We see, then, that the term Zion referring to the people of Israel is eternal, applicable even in Galuth and not restricted by geography, while

## Zionism, Judaism, and Eretz Yisroel

the term Zion, referring to the land of Israel, is a particular national one. It follows therefore, that Zionism is not synonymous with Judaism, as many were moved to proclaim recently, but rather an integral, important aspect of Judaism. It certainly is diminished by being called the National Liberation movement of the Jewish people, a term so cherished by emerging third world people. This is pandering to popular taste. Eretz Yisroel, and our historic rights to it, are part of the covenant with the Almighty wherein we are granted the Holy Land in keeping with the promise made to the patriarchs beginning with Abraham. This is the only answer to a world which questions our legitimacy and it is important for every Jew to recognize it if he is to find his authentic identity, for only with integrity can identity be realized.

How to view Jewish nationalism is the most serious challenge confronting the state and the Jewish people since 1948. Because the power structure and leadership elite in Israel have been largely insensitive to the Torah concept of Jewish nationalism, a generation has been reared which interprets our national destiny no different from that of other people. A young man who was totally assimilated recently wrote that he was brought back to the Jewish fold through his identification with Zionism and the State of Israel. At the end of his touching confession, he makes the following statement "we are a nation, once again, at long last." How unfortunate that his understanding of Jewish history is so impoverished that he cannot comprehend that we were a nation even before the State of Israel was established in 1948. A secular interpretation of Jewish nationalism also breeds the erroneous idea that our existence is dependent entirely upon the might of our own hands and the superiority of the Israeli military establishment. A leading official of the Ministry of Education addressing a Chanukah gathering at Modin stated — "like the Maccabees of old, we have none to rely upon except ourselves," which is not only an arrogant statement but also a distortion of Jewish history. It is most disturbing that a top Israeli educator is so unaware of the Maccabees' trust in the Almighty and their belief that only with the help of Heaven were they successful in their battles.

Even in the aftermath of the Yom Kippur war, which to a degree deflated the Israeli ego, the vast majority of Jewish leaders still viewed the State of Israel and the national destiny of the people of

## Zionism, Judaism, and Eretz Yisroel

Israel, in a spirit contrary to that projected in the Torah, the Prophets and our Sages. The admonition of Ezekiel sums up the philosophy of Jewish tradition in defining the historical role of Israel. "And that which cometh into your mind shall not be at all, in that ye say we will be as the nations, as the families of the countries. As I live, sayeth the Lord, surely with a mighty hand and an outstretched hand . . . will I be King over you." Long before Ezekiel, a heathen prophet, Bilaam, expressed the classic position of Judaism regarding Israel's uniqueness and her relationship with other nations. "Behold, a people that dwell alone," anticipates Israel's isolation just as Ezekiel's statement foresees the special destiny and role of Israel. The question is whether Jews are sufficiently mature and wise to accept this challenging role with equanimity, courage, and faith. To the Torah Jew it is not only our fate to be alone but our glory as well. To the secular-oriented Jewish nationalist, it is a tragedy and calamity.

Time, however, has brought these two camps closer together in their point of view and conception of Jewish destiny. Twenty-eight years of independence has brought Israel neither acceptance nor 'normalcy.' Israel has in recent years been unable to retain the initial sympathy of the world and the unequivocal support of its Western friends, by appealing to their conscience to rectify the sins of the Holocaust or by pointing to its credentials as a brave little island of democracy in a sea of oppressive undemocratic countries.

The United Nations resolution on Zionism paradoxically had some positive aspects as well as negative results. It forced many in the secular camp to respond in a traditional manner for the first time since the establishment of the state. Justification for our presence in the land of Israel, and our legitimacy as a nation, were presented from platforms and in written articles as based upon the mandate of the Bible, and our claims to this ancient land upon the Divine covenant — precisely the arguments used for so many years by the traditionalists! At times it is our enemies, strangely, who are the instruments of soul-searching and the irritants for discovery of our authentic, historic roots and rights.

Even non-religious Jews reacted favorably when Jewish spokesmen finally stated boldly and publicly that our rights to the land of Israel are not based upon the kindness and beneficence of the world community, but is the will of the Almighty granted to us as

## Zionism, Judaism, and Eretz Yisroel

part of an ancient Divine covenant. This was also enthusiastically echoed by many in the Christian world reflecting their reverence for the Bible and respect for the historic claim of the Children of Israel.

In spite of the ideological and philosophical shortcomings of Israeli leadership during the past quarter century, the mystical magnetism of the land of Israel still holds sway. Even Jews who have little or no commitment to Torah and mitzvoth, and in many cases have become assimilated into the non-Jewish society and culture, still retain a strong sense of devotion to the State of Israel. A non-Jew once referred to this strange phenomenon as 'ancestral alchemy' and, indeed, the Holy Land does have this unusual quality of transforming base metal into gold, Jewishly speaking. For the citizens of Israel this magic has a tendency to work when most needed, overcoming the doubts and fears to which they have been subjected since the birth of the state. Witness the electrifying rescue operation of the IDF at Entebbe, which renewed Israel's self-assurance and self-respect at a time when their morale was at such a low ebb. Still, many problems prevail.

The problems besetting Israel at the present time are manifold. The euphoria of the post-Six-Day War period began evaporating in the early 70s and was completely dissipated by the Yom Kippur War. In response to the question I posed to many government and religious leaders last year, "What was the single most important effect of the Yom Kippur War upon the Israelis?" the answer without exception was *shock*. Until the Yom Kippur war of 1973, Israelis were convinced that the Arabs would never initiate a war. The realization that the Arab world was still sufficiently motivated to launch a military attack, compounded with the recognition that Israeli invincibility was a myth, resulted in a state of shock which still lingers three years later. As Minister Burg put it, "Israel had a military victory in '73 but suffered a psychological defeat."

There are a number of realities which must be confronted. Jews throughout the world must not romanticize about Israel, and all of us must face up to these new realities which are threefold. One is ongoing Arab intransigence and their stubborn determination not to accept the historic fact of Israel as a permanent fixture in the Middle East. The second reality is the tremendous world-wide power wielded by the Arab states through the weapon of oil and petro dollars, a power which the Arabs themselves did not realize they possessed until the oil boycott and price increase imposed after the Yom Kippur War. The third cause for alarm is the changing attitude of the western world, including the United States, toward Israel and the Arab countries. Isolated diplomatically, economically, and politically, Israel can ill afford to lose its one major powerful friend and, therefore, must find ways to accommodate the new United States policy of "even handedness" while not compromising its national security.

Prime Minister Rabin made a very incisive observation at the Jewish Agency Assembly held in Jerusalem last year, which was not properly appreciated by most political analysts. He revealed that during his visit to Washington, he told President Ford that Israel had accomplished military victories on the battlefield four times in the past twenty-five years only to be denied the fruits of these victories, namely a political settlement. He told Mr. Ford quite candidly that the reason a political settlement has been denied Israel was due to the intervention of the major powers, at times the United States and other times, Russia. This perceptive anslysis of Mr. Rabin serves to underscore the truth of the old adage that "small states do not have a foreign policy, only foreign relations." The Yom Kippur War served to remind Israel that we cannot rely exclusively upon the might of our arms while the post-Yom Kippur diplomatic maneuvering reminds us that we cannot rely upon traditional political friends and allies when they are convinced that their nation's self-interests will best be served by wooing Israel's enemies, even at the expense of Israel's own security.

As these three major problems confront Israel externally, so there are three major areas of concern internally which merit our attention. They are first, the morale of the people, their self-assurance, inner strength and stamina. Second, the social fabric and collective character of Israeli society today, and finally, the religious spirit and collective soul of the Israeli community.

The mood in Israel today is a disturbing one. One has but to examine the 1975 statistics of immigration vs. emigration to appreciate the great problem confronting world Jewry, and above all the Israeli government. For the first time since the establishment of the state, the number of *olim* and *yordim* were practically equal. Western "aliyah" has been reduced to a trickle and the Russian "aliyah" is also radically diminished. Potential western *olim* are dissuaded by a number of factors. There is great anxiety and apprehension due to the unstable political and military situation in Israel, compounded by periodic terrorist attacks. Runaway inflation has deterred many who may have contemplated aliyah in the realization that even though the dollar buys more Israeli pounds, the pounds in turn buy far less than they did in the past. The recent economic recession in the United States has also served to divert the attention of American Jews from plans of aliyah to attempts to recoup their losses so that they may at some future date emigrate to Israel in a position of financial strength.

Russian emigration has been drastically curtailed by the Soviet government, but even among those who are permitted to leave far too many have chosen to emigrate to lands other than Israel. There is a twofold reason for this disappointing trend. One is that strongly-motivated Zionist Jews have already left Russia, while those presently leaving are not as Zionistically or Jewishly inclined. A second reason is that many Russian *olim* are dissatisfied with Israel and have been sending letters back to Russia dissuading their family and friends from joining them. This dissatisfaction is due to the fact that many Russian Jews anticipated coming to a land which literally flows with milk and honey, only to find that the period of adjustment and absorption is a long and difficult one. Their exaggerated expectations were shattered by the harsh realities of Israel's problems resulting in a negative effect upon more recent Russian emigrées. A prominent Israeli rabbi told me "these people are filled with animosity for Communism and become ultra-capitalistic, obsessed with the desire for material things and private possessions which they expected to find immediately upon their arrival in Israel. Unless they get the best apartments, a well-paying job and a TV set at once, they feel that they have been misled and cheated."

The problem of diminished immigration has been compounded by an alarming increase of "yeridah," emigration from Israel, including native-born Israelis. The difficult times confronting Israel is indeed putting the nation to a serious test as to how deep are their roots in the land of Israel and how lasting their commitment to the state. As one government leader put it to me "Let's face it. How deep are the roots of Jews who came here from Morocco twenty years ago, from Roumania twelve years ago, and from Russia three years ago?" Unfortunately this is true of "sabras" as well. It is gratifying to note that those Jews who came on "aliyah" motivated by their religious faith and love for the Promised Land have proven to be the most loyal to the State of Israel. Be they from Yemen, the United States, South Africa or Georgian-Russian Jews, they are far less prone to becoming "yordim" than secular Zionist-oriented immigrants. The same is true of native-born Israelis. Those who have received a Torah education have proven to be far more loyal and committed to the land than those who have received a secular Israeli education.

In fairness to wavering Israelis, one must appreciate that there are many disrupting factors which cause individuals and families to become frustrated and despairing, motivating them to leave for other countries. Consider but one area and you can understand why Israelis entertain the thought of "yeridah." We refer to the requirement to serve as a reservist in the army well into middle age which demands leaving one's job and family for a minimum of 45 days each year. What happens to a man's business or profession while he absents himself for this period of time during the course of the year? What emotional effect does this have upon his wife and children, when the husband and father is away so often? Consider also the depressing effect upon Israelis, young and old alike, exposed constantly to streets filled with soldiers in uniform, Uzi or rifle slung over their shoulders, and civilian guards on the streets every evening with rifle in hand. Israel has become, to a great extent, a garrison state with all the resultant psychological problems. Peoples' attitudes and values are perforce affected by such pressures and it's unfair for those who live in other comparatively tranquil countries to judge their brethren who must live under these difficult conditions. If anything, our admiration for those who remain should be increased, especially when one rides through the Negev and Golan Heights and witnesses the hundreds upon hundreds of young people who have established settlements in these desolate areas.

The social fabric and collective character of Israel is the second area of concern. In the early years of the state, one was impressed by the spirit of optimism and genuine idealism which marked Israeli society. The materialistic spirit of the Western world had not as yet penetrated or overwhelmed the citizens of this newly-reborn country. Although there were people of varied backgrounds arriving in Israel, each with their own language, culture and life style, resulting in a heterogeneous community, nonetheless the unifying factors of common hopes and aspirations were sufficiently strong to serve as a cementing force. The excitement of establishing a Jewish state generated an enthusiasm and commitment which enabled people to transcend many problems.

With the passage of time, however, idealism tended to wane and the materialistic spirit of America and Western Europe made heavy inroads into Israeli society. German reparation money also contributed to a frantic pursuit of possessions. Publications and movies, awakened new appetites and desires in the minds of many and the post-Six-Day War euphoria helped to contribute to the pursuit of pleasure. All this resulted in radical changes affecting the Israeli's sense of values, attitudes and life style. The shock of the Yom Kippur War was not of sufficient magnitude to alter the moral and ethical climate, nor did it have a lasting impact upon the Israeli's scale of values. Although the economy is hurting and inflation more serious than that of other countries, nonetheless, most people's desire for luxury items has not abated and the majority are living beyond their means. Sensitive, perceptive Israeli leaders are concerned about the moral climate which has deteriorated and the Chief Rabbi told me that his greatest anguish and worry lies in the fact that he observes a moral and ethical erosion which unfortunately matches that of the Western world.

Although there is a tendency to exaggerate shortcomings in Israel, since we expect such high standards from the Holy Land, nonetheless these problems are real. The only hope lies in the strengthening of education and the increased influence of spiritual and moral leadership which is regrettably quite ineffective and impotent. The Yeshiva and Torah world are still bright areas, especially Yeshivoth Hesder, whose students and graduates have captured the imagination of many and made a deep, positive impression upon Israelis of all political parties. These young men who are observant, study Torah, and excel in their army service, are looked to as the dynamic leaders of the future who will play a vital role and inject their spirit into the general society. Unfortunately, many of these young men are not interested in serving as rabbis since the Rabbinate in general, has not established itself as a prestigious profession. Fortunately, they are interested in education and the standards of many religious-oriented schools will eventually be elevated by the infusion of this new breed.

The educational structure in Israel is a baffling one which can only be appreciated by parents of school-age children who must decide where to enroll their sons and daughters. The multitude of schools; secular-government, religious-government, independent-religious network of schools (Chinuch Atzmai) as well as the many Chasidic-oriented schools present a most confusing picture to the uninitiated. It is clear, however, that those schools located in middle- and upper-class Ashkenazic communities have a much higher standard than those situated in poorer Sephardic neighborhoods. The caliber of teachers also determines the quality of each school regardless of their affiliation and label, thereby resulting in the strange phenomenon of many American "olim" who are lifelong Zionists sending their children to the Agudist sponsored Chinuch Atzmai schools, while non-Mizrachi parents send their children to certain religious-government schools because of the high quality of their teaching staff and curriculum standards.

Ashkenazi-Sephardi tensions are still present and since the Sephardim are now the majority of the population, they are progressively more impatient with their lot and status. Their economic level is by and large below that of the Ashkenazim and they feel most deeply that they are not afforded sufficient recognition or granted proper positions in government and the private sector. Fortunately, many more Sephardim are attending the universities and they have begun to serve in more important government positions. There has also been an increase of Sephardic officers in the Israeli army. The educational arena is a most difficult one with de facto segregation in many schools due to neighborhood and economic reasons. When integration is attempted, there is often a lowering of educational standards. It is interesting to note that the same problems which beset us in the United States confront the Israelis as well and will take some time to solve.

As for the religious community, the elusive blessing of unity, harmony, and peace still escapes them. The rift within the Torah world cannot be ignored. If anything, there has been a hardening of positions. Two forces now become clearly recognizable and definable, even within the Yeshiva world. A visitor is amazed at certain phrases used to depict the various elements within the Yeshiva world, such as "Black Hat Yeshiva" as opposed to "Kipah Serugah" schools. What divides them is not only the question "to serve or not to serve" in the army, but, in general, their attitude toward the total Israeli society. The centrists, usually identified with the Mizrachi movement and the B'nai Akiva movement, are totally involved in Israeli society and devoted patriotic citizens of the state. This does not mean they are uncritical and unquestioning, but their loyalty and commitment is beyond reproach. Those who identify with Agudah and the traditional Yeshiva world are far more critical, less fervent in their support of the government, and more isolated from the general community. One must be careful to note, however, that even in the so-called "right wing" there are many who involve themselves with the community and are concerned for the development of Israeli society beyond their own parochial area, while there are young men of the Hesder Yeshivoth and Mizrachi adherents who play a minimal role in the mainstream of society.

The channels of communication between these two traditional segments are comparatively closed and this lack of unity within the orthodox community has weakened its impact and influence upon Israeli society. Most intelligent observers agree that non-observant Israelis will continue to be suspicious of the motivations of traditional Jewry as long as they believe that every religious issue is politically motivated. They also will continue to be wary of orthodox impositions upon them, such as Sabbath observance, Kashruth, and other "restrictions." Looking into the future, one is prone to agree with those who argue that it is vital to establish an independent orthodox force divorced from the political parties, which can gain the confidence of the non-observant and attract the many Israelis who have become disillusioned with their own political ideologies and are sincerely interested in finding their Jewish roots and traditions. There is a great reservoir of talent to be found in the Torah world and when this will be tapped, it will doubtless prove to be a tremendous force for good in the State of Israel.

All these international and domestic problems besetting Israel have not succeeded, fortunately, in subduing the spirit of the people. The vast majority of Israelis are determined to follow the advice given by Ben Gurion many years ago, "no illusions, no despair."

The courage and bravery demonstrated so often by our brethren in Israel arouses our love and admiration. The apt saying that "to love is to admire with the heart and to admire is to love with the mind" captures the feeling of world Jewry regarding the State of Israel. The recent epic rescue mission in Uganda on July 4, 1976, demonstrated once again that Israel cares profoundly for the safety and welfare of their citizens and refuses to be intimidated, as do unfortunately, much greater powers in the face of terrorism. This glorious episode also served to remind us that "Behold, the Guardian of Israel neither slumbers nor sleeps." Miracles in our day are hidden not revealed, yet who did not see in this mission the miraculous assistance of Divine providence? The passage of time serves but to prove the wisdom of another remark made by Ben Gurion regarding the amazing development of the new State, "whoever does not believe in miracles is not a realist."

The believing Jew sees the hand of the Almighty constantly manifested in the destiny of Israel and in events as they develop in the countries which encircle and threaten Israel's very existence. Consider for example, the unfolding bizarre drama in Lebanon where we witness Syria, Israel's fiercest antagonist in the north, battling the P.L.O., Israel's mortal enemy! This is so illogical and difficult for the world to understand that we are inspired to echo the ancient words of our Sages "the Almighty has at His behest many messengers." We constantly see that the promise given in the time of Samuel "G-d will not forsake His people," has been reconfirmed in the history of Eretz Yisroel during the past quarter century.

There are many issues which divide Jews in our time. Commitment to Torah, observance of Mitzvoth and even basic loyalty to K'lal Yisroel has eroded. There is, however, one unifying force which has demonstrated its power to evoke the emotional response and support of the vast majority of Jews — the State of Israel. Even when the covenant of Torah is neglected by so many, the ancient vow made at the rivers of Babylon has not been violated, "If I forget thee O' Jerusalem may my right hand forget its cunning." It is this eternal oath which has kept alive the love of Jews for their homeland close to two thousand years of exile and it is this vow which will, G-d willing, insure the existence and vitality of Medinat Yisroel until the advent of *Moshiach* and the *Geulah Shelemah*.